How a Global Pandemic Changed the Way We Travel

How a Global Pandemic Changed the Way We Travel

Jacqueline Jeynes

BEP

BUSINESS EXPERT PRESS

Leader in applied, concise business books

Description

At the end of 2019, COVID-19 spread rapidly around the world to become a global pandemic. Tourism and hospitality sectors were particularly hard hit with a virtual halt to travel, internally and across borders, with constantly changing rules intended to restrict movement and safeguard travelers. Throughout this period, we have tracked reactions by people, health advisors, and politicians worldwide, as infection rates and deaths from the virus rose or fell dramatically.

We explore how travel and tourism have been affected—both leisure and business travel; safeguards introduced to protect people and the planet; and whether this has resulted in permanent change to the way we travel in the future. For many within the industry, it has been an opportunity to review every aspect of global travel and to define a "new normal" for the future.

Keywords

travel; tourism; hospitality; leisure travel; business travel; COVID-19 virus; global pandemic; infection rates and deaths from COVID-19; vaccination programs; lockdowns; essential travel; all travel suspended; the Bucket List; traffic light system for safe destinations; enforced quarantine; future travel restrictions; travel agents; reopening visitor attractions; changing how we make bookings

Contents

Foreword

At the beginning of 2020, travel and tourism sectors were a growing, thriving industry. Mature travelers were seen as the ones with more disposable income, wanting to take two to three holidays/trips each year and looking for new experiences globally. Younger age groups were more likely to plan a trip at shorter notice, often preferring social media platforms that included UGIs (user-generated images) and positive influencer feedback.

Going forward two years, it was clear that the COVID-19 pandemic had completely changed options for travel and, indeed, views of individuals about how/where/whether to travel outside their home country. The excitement and spontaneity of poring over a map and choosing a new destination, as in Figure F.1, may take a bit longer to resurface.

Looking back at travel and tourism, we can see how restrictions introduced around the world impacted on everyone's views of where they

Figure F.1 Planning a trip

could visit. This overview of how options for travel changed leads directly to where we want to be as we get used to a new form of "normal." While no one is sure at what stage the pandemic becomes an endemic disease—more like the usual flu occurring in "seasonal or predictable cycles" (E.Murray Boston University) and therefore we have some sort of control over it—it will be a while before all precautions can be relaxed. It is important, therefore, to identify the critical issues that must be addressed if travel and tourism sectors are to survive in the future.

Introduction

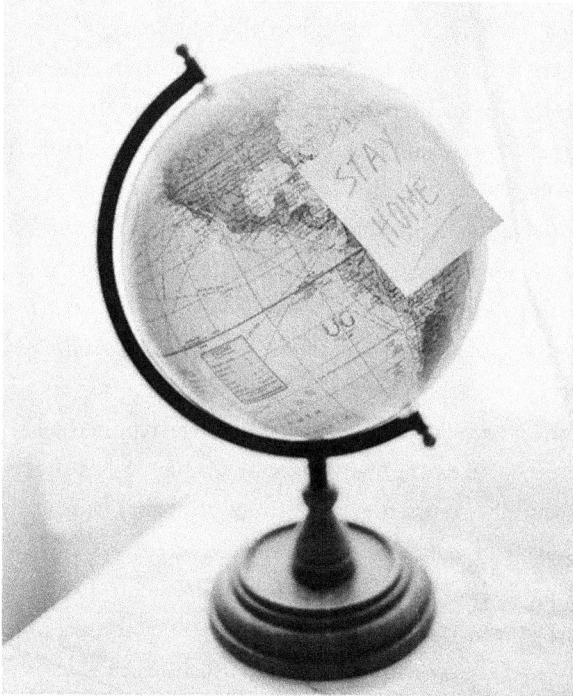

Figure I.1 The world is closed to visitors

> *It is difficult to define the tourism industry—in its broadest sense, [it] is defined as when people travel and stay in places outside of their usual environment for less than one consecutive year for leisure, business, health, or other reasons.*
>
> —Definition of tourism (Statista February 2022)

How we define "tourism" is never going to be a simple exercise as it includes so many different elements of product or service. The statement above is a good summary as we can recognize the basic principles behind it. So, with this definition in mind, we can look at the major changes taking place since 2019, consider how these have directly affected how we travel, and be prepared for when the world is once more open to visitors (Figure I.1).

As with the previous book by the author (JJ), the latest available sources are used to help draw a realistic picture of the industry: for example, Silver Travel Advisor surveys (120,000+ members), ADARA marketing surveys, international statistics, and media stories and coverage. However, this is to underpin discussion in the book rather than be an academic thesis as the ordinary, individual traveler is just as interested in these issues as those in the tourism and hospitality sectors or those studying the impact of the pandemic.

When the author's previous book, *Targeting the Mature Traveler,* was written, views about future travel trends were emerging although the true impact of the pandemic was still not recognized. This book, *How a Global Pandemic Changed the Way We Travel,* builds on that publication, with data from major players in the travel and marketing sectors who seek to inform tourism providers. Where surveys were repeated with the same target groups, such as the mature sector through Silver Travel Advisor, the optimism for a return to some form of normality had clearly waned.

The global pandemic completely changed the way we live, work, and travel during 2020–2021 with the full impact into 2022 and beyond still unclear. There have always been significant outbreaks of contagious illnesses around the world, and we have usually been able to contain or control them to a greater or lesser extent. Rather than "stunning us with one catastrophic event," as Dan Richards of Global Rescue pointed out in early 2020 (Washington Post), the virus surprised us all with its determination to reach into every aspect of our life.

This time, it was very different as it represented a truly global pandemic rather than one restricted to a particular region (however far it reached within that area). So, a rapidly changing unknown that, given its spread around the globe, resulted in difficult medical and political decisions across nations.

Although the book is written as restrictions are lifting and the industry begins to recover, it has far-reaching implications for all of us. What has changed since the beginning of 2020 when COVID-19 was suddenly recognized as more virulent than expected?

At that time, the travel market was growing; people were planning to take more trips each year in the future, especially mature travelers with growing numbers in 50+ age group starting to look at different options. Globally, travel and tourism contributed more than US$4.5 trillion to GDP (gross domestic product) and, in some countries, was the main contributor.

Throughout the book, we will look more closely at the impact on individuals and businesses; how hospitality, travel, and tourism were hardest hit; and critical questions we need to ask potential travelers in order to survive and bounce back in the future. While some options may be temporary or short-lived, there have clearly been far-reaching and fundamental changes to the way we travel. It is important, therefore, that future provision takes into account different expectations of both leisure and business travelers in the future.

Crucial issues for the industry going forward into 2022 and beyond include:

- Changes for the individual when planning and booking a trip.
- Is the "staycation" likely to stay as a popular option or will people still want to travel overseas?
- How has the "Bucket List" changed (if at all) given views on overtourism and environmental damage?
- What actions have those in tourism sectors taken to address these issues or are planning to take in the future?
- How has business travel changed and will it go back to previous levels?

The situation with COVID-19 is, of course, ongoing and ever-changing, but people will continue to want and need to travel in some way whatever the final decisions about containing the virus or finding a way to live with it. The question is, will it revert to how it was or will we have to accept that what we do, where we go, and how we get there will change to a completely new reality.

SECTION 1

The Impact of the Pandemic

CHAPTER 1

The Way We Were

After two years of highs and lows in dealing with the pandemic, it is useful to look back at how things were at the beginning of 2020 and the fundamental changes that have taken place since then. As one of the hardest hit sectors, and the basis of how we spend our leisure or work time, a look at how our views about travel have changed is a timely activity.

There was growing recognition of the virus becoming a major "pandemic" as large numbers of people were affected by COVID-19; there was a surge in the number of deaths associated with it and a growing realization of how quickly it could spread. It was clear it was "not just the flu," but a particularly virulent strain even though its basic structure was similar. We soon came to recognize the colorful, graphical representation of what it looked like as it was presented in all the news broadcasts around the world (Figure 1.1). The hardest hit countries at the start of the pandemic included China, Italy, Spain, United States, and South America, but other countries soon saw a fast growth in the numbers affected.

A Demographic Picture

In relation to the impact of the COVID-19 pandemic, it will be interesting to see how the demographic profiles have changed worldwide when data are available from 2022 onwards. However, with any demographic statistics, there are significant differences globally and in the way they are collated. For instance, two major sources of data include Worldometers and Statista who both collate data in distinct categories making it difficult to make any meaningful comparisons.

In 2020, the Worldometers world demographic summaries show (www.worldometers.info/demographic):

- Over 40 percent of the population was in the age group 0 to 24.
- Over 40 percent of the population was in the age group 25 to 54.
- Nearly 20 percent of the population was aged 55+.

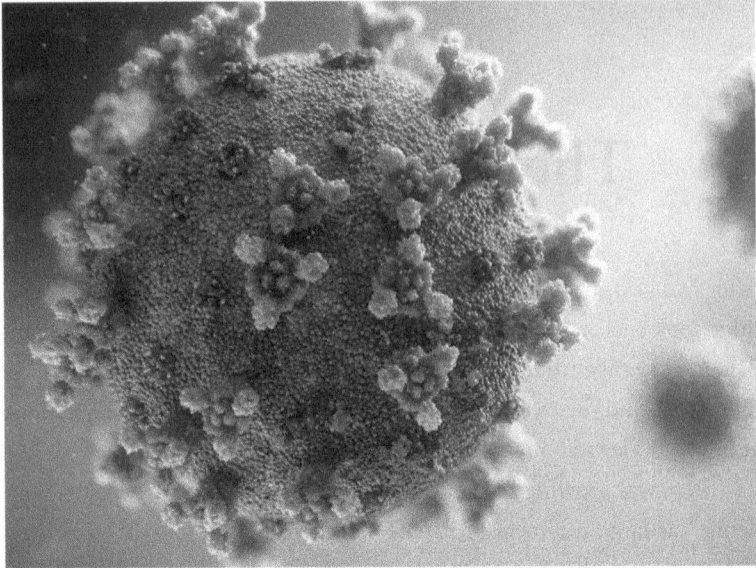

Figure 1.1 The COVID-19 virus

In 2021, the Statista world demographics show (www.statista.com):

- 26 percent under 15 years of age
- 10 percent 65+

Compared with the global breakdowns, various sources show that in 2020 there were twice as many people in the United Kingdom in the 65+ bracket, and three times as many in this bracket in Japan. The 2021 profile for Europe shows 16 percent are under 15 years old and 19 percent age 65+, with an even spread across these age groups in North America. While these demographic profiles play a part in how we track increases in travel numbers, and the way each age group sees the impact of the virus on their travel plans, the lack of consistency in categorizing demographic groups makes it more difficult to forecast and plan for the future at a global level. How you define the "mature" market is a good example: 50+? 60+? 75+?

There are different versions of how we can define age groups, particularly for baby boomers as including those born up to 1980 means they are the children of baby boomers. However you choose to define them, some indications of what different age groups are looking for in relation to travel are helpful. For this book, we go with the following broad categories.

Baby boomers: Part of the boom in birth rates following WWII when numbers surged to a million. They are the mature travelers of today. Born between 1945 and 1950s, this group is often extended to include those born before 1966.

Generation X: Children of original baby boomers—1966 to 1980
Generation Y: Millennials—1980 to end of 1990s
Generation Z (this definition varies): 1990s to 2000

The Travel Sector Before the Pandemic

At the start of the pandemic, around three-quarters of mature travelers were taking at least three trips each year, while the younger age groups who were employed, and therefore had fewer opportunities to take time away from the workplace, aimed to have one major vacation/holiday with another shorter break outside school term times. As we will see later, the pandemic resulted in a significant shift in when and how trips could be planned.

By the middle of 2020, there was still a fairly upbeat view of future travel, with regular studies to suggest how things were changing due to COVID-19. Despite this, the U.S. Travel Association (USTA) stated that since March 2020, there had been over $500 billion cumulative losses for the U.S. economy, and the United Nations World Travel Organization (UNWTO) believed the value of the decline in international tourism to be between $910 billion and $1.2 trillion as lost revenue. Given such substantial numbers, it is questionable whether the sector could ever recover such losses. Looking back at some of these early views, we can see how unprepared the world was for the true extent of the restrictions that were being introduced and how long they would need to be in place.

The Washington Post was one of the earliest to do so, identifying a list of "11 Ways the Pandemic Will Change Travel" in June 2020 (WP). Referring to "Revenge Travel" as the way to get over the pandemic, people were convinced that as confidence was growing stronger and they believed that the threat to their safety was reducing, they were ready to start planning their next trip for 2021. Note the emphasis was on domestic travel in the United States, rather than going overseas, and a belief in the developing vaccine program worldwide.

This did not fit exactly with government advice and health requirements for travel at the time, so it was an optimistic view. In addition, there was concern that crossing U.S. state borders may not be so easy as each was able to introduce its own COVID-19 safety precautions. There might also be differences in what venues could stay open and the numbers of people who can visit. For instance, in 2020, Hawaii and Maine required visitors to quarantine for 14 days on arrival or show negative COVID-19 test results (WP).

In the United Kingdom, as the first lockdown restrictions started to ease, people in all age groups were keen to book a vacation as soon as possible. Although older travelers remained determined in their aim to travel again as soon as possible, this was based on their belief in the vaccination programs being rolled out globally. There was "a growing enthusiasm to get vaccinated and get back out there again" (STA).

Remember, the 60+ age group was identified early on as the most vulnerable to the most severe impact of the virus. This was the first group advised to self-isolate—basically, to stay at home. Yet this is the group that previously traveled more often, especially overseas, and was keen to explore new experiences. For instance, this group represented 60 percent of travel and tourism spent in the United Kingdom, £2.2 billion more than millennials.

Surveys also showed that almost half of the respondents expected to take a trip before the end of 2020. The difference was that the distances they planned to travel had certainly shrunk, with the majority saying it would be in the home country rather than overseas. Insurance companies saw a similar picture with policies for domestic trips rising to 48 percent from the usual 15 percent (Squaremouth comparison site), and hotel booking site Travelocity seeing most trips within 100 miles of home. As we see later, the staycation is already starting to grow as an option for many travelers.

The biggest obstacles to long-distance travel were concerns over insurance cover related to COVID-19 problems and the ever-changing quarantine restrictions. This continued to be an issue in 2022, as confirmed by

Debbie Marshall, original founder of Silver Travel Advisor site and now Silver Marketing Association:

> There is no doubt that the pandemic has made some people (of all ages) more cautious about travelling. The fear of getting stuck in another country if the rules change suddenly, the concern about contracting Covid whilst overseas and then not being able to return to the UK, or requiring medical treatment, are the main issues. (Debbie Marshall (SMA) 2022)

Short flights were becoming more popular than long-haul flights to far-off destinations. In the older 70+ age groups, the belief in protection through vaccination on such flights was not an issue as around a third said they would never fly long-haul again.

Awareness of damage to the environment due to long-haul flights and traveling long distances from your home base were already growing, as was the need to be more eco-friendly wherever you visit, now a stronger element of choice for travelers and therefore forcing a rethink by tour operators.

Although the Bucket List was still a significant element when people were deciding where to go—note this was increasingly more important for younger 45+ age groups too—demand for different destinations and activities was emerging. Overtourism had to be considered in order to slow the damage to the most popular destinations across the globe, including cities like Amsterdam or attractions such as Machu Picchu. Another useful definition is that of UNWTO who define overtourism as:

> The impact of tourism on a destination, or parts thereof, that excessively influences perceived quality of life of citizens and/or quality of visitor experiences, in a negative way.

All feedback from surveys at the time showed a consistent picture of how and why views about the pandemic changed and would affect everyone's future travel plans.

CHAPTER 2

What Changed

Although views held by the public and the conditions imposed by governments varied around the world, there were general patterns emerging. It was accepted that those in the worst-hit countries, trying to deal with a spike in deaths from the virus, lived in a more precarious situation, which also added to the general feeling of confusion.

How the Pandemic Was Viewed in 2020

Going back through statements made internationally during the first six months of 2020, we can see how confused everyone was about COVID-19 and how serious it was for the population of all ages. Table 2.1 summarizes the statements made in the press during the first half of 2020.

By June 2020, millions of jobs were at risk in hospitality and travel sectors, and the USTA stated that a third of all jobs lost in the United States was in the travel industry. As borders closed and lockdowns began on a massive scale, everyone was confused about what rules and regulations applied to them in their location. As the focus was on saving lives, with people largely confined to their own home, a financial disaster was inevitable.

Bad loans already totaled £2.1 billion in the United Kingdom alone, there was an estimated £105 billion of unsustainable business debt, and household spending had dropped by more than 40 percent. The statement by Robert Chote from the Office for Budget Responsibility that "the economy is over the worst of the crisis" (despite it shrinking by 35 percent already) was clearly a bit optimistic!

From the middle of 2020 until the early part of 2022, there were more developments as we saw spikes in the rates of infections and deaths from COVID-19 and governments tried to find ways to deal with the ongoing pandemic.

Table 2.1 Public statements quoted directly in many newspapers and TV broadcasts

February 2020	World Health Organization (WHO) refused to declare the crisis a "pandemic" despite the growing death toll, but even at this early point U.S. Centers for Disease Control and Prevention (CDC) warned it was a case of "when" not "if" it would be seen as a pandemic. By February 28, 2020, WHO chief Tedros Adhanom Ghebreyesus reported that "This virus has pandemic potential, we're at a decisive point"
	Countries that reported their first cases included Norway, Greece, Brazil, Algeria, and the United Kingdom. Italy was identified as a "Danger Zone" as 12 had died but numbers were rising rapidly
	Vulnerable groups were identified as those with existing medical conditions and those over 70 as they were likely to suffer the most severe effects; 15% of those over 80 years old who got the virus died, but at that time no children had died
	Patterns were starting to emerge as more men than women died from the virus
	By February 27, there were over 81,000 cases reported and 2,771 deaths. However, in the United Kingdom, the government stated that "If a pandemic is declared here [we are] unlikely to close borders, stop mass gatherings, shut down public transport"
March 2020	Emergency Nightingale hospitals were being set up to cater for a surge in the number of COVID cases and it was accepted that this was "a significant challenge" and the "worst public health crisis in a generation"
	The public was shocked to see images of exhausted hospital staff lying asleep on the corridor floors, and shortages in PPE were being reported globally
	First lockdown announced in the United Kingdom; U.K. furlough (CJRS) scheme introduced
	German short-time working allowance covered 10 million workers; U.S. FPUC scheme paid more than 30 million workers; in France, the Chomage Partiel scheme covered workers unable to work; Ireland had a temporary wage subsidy scheme
April 2020	In the United Kingdom, 413 deaths were recorded in one day and the total deaths there were 20,732. Many of these were paramedics, care home staff, postal workers, and police officers, and at least 20 bus drivers had died
	By the end of April, it was identified that people of color and those from minority ethnic groups (in the United Kingdom) were dying at a greater rate than the rest of the population. However, this was not just a straightforward statistic as poverty was a critical factor—poor white people were also dying at a greater rate than the general population
	Lockdown was still in place as it was seen as too risky to ease restrictions yet
	UBS believed 20% independent eateries would close permanently

May 2020	There had been 26,771 deaths in the United Kingdom at the beginning of May, 28,446 by May 4, and 31,241 by the end of the week; 12 children had died from the virus, 66% of deaths had been men, with most fatalities in those aged 20–64 years
	It was identified that those in lower-skilled jobs were four times more likely to die from the virus, and security operatives or taxi/cab drivers were five times more likely to die if they caught the virus
	Countries with the most deaths at this time were the United States around 68,000; the United Kingdom and Italy nearly 29,000; France with more than 24,000
	Germany had a spike of 300 new cases among meat factory workers. The latest outbreak in South Korea was traced back to a nightclub
	Surprisingly, WHO chief scientist stated that shops and schools could "safely" reopen now as the "experts know how to keep coronavirus under control." However, they later stated the pandemic was far from over with 106,000 new cases reported in the previous 24 hours
	There had been no big outbreaks in schools around the world, but Germany found that 4,000 coronavirus patients and children were infected so no schools were opened. Infection rates were growing in Latin America with Brazil in third place for the number of confirmed cases worldwide
	There were positive results from the United States concerning the vaccine it was developing
	In Germany, the number of confirmed cases rose to 160,758 with 6,481 deaths. It had hoped to open large venues and visitor attractions such as galleries and zoos but decided to put this on hold
	Despite the growing number of cases and deaths, there were still people refusing to believe it was a pandemic ("just a cold or the normal flu they said") with demonstrations against continuing lockdown. Note that Sweden now had the worst death rate per million in the world as they said no to any lockdown
	The number of deaths in the United Kingdom was now the highest in Europe and it was noted that clearly this was not a short-term crisis but "large epidemic waves" could be expected in the future
June 2020	By June, the CDC in the United States was saying that numbers of hospitalizations and infection rates were reducing, so feeding the impression that the worst of the pandemic might be over
	USTA stated $500 billion cumulative losses for the United States; a third of jobs lost in the country were in travel industry (USTA); *Washington Post* referred to "Revenge Travel" as belief in reducing threat to safety
	Hawaii and Maine required 14 days quarantine for visitors on arrival
	Traffic light system introduced in the United Kingdom to list safe destinations
	Crime rates reduced by around 25%; sharp rise in domestic violence cases

Table 2.2 Public statements about the impact of the pandemic

November 2020	Threat seen as greater to the country than the individual
	Lockdowns reintroduced worldwide; U.K. lockdown ended beginning December but other restrictions still in force. Tier systems introduced
	90% of event planners had lost some or all of their business; 21% believed smaller meetings would be the most common in the future
	During 2020, 6 million cruise passengers compared with 30 million in 2019
January 2021	England in third lockdown
February 2021	NASA released images of reduced emissions in China during lockdowns
	SAGA holidays required all passengers to have had both vaccines
Spring 2021	German nationals were allowed to travel to other European countries
	Nonessential shops and services allowed to reopen
	Table service only in bars and restaurants
	Free lateral flow tests widely available in the United Kingdom
	Tourists started to travel across county/state borders even if from high-risk areas
	Lockdowns reintroduced
	USTA stated business travel would not recover until 2024; business travel spending down 76%—$97 billion loss
July 2021	Bookings in the United Kingdom for trips overseas were 65% higher than June as Amber List destinations announced; 40% rise in bookings for Croatia and Malta (on safe list) and around a third for Sri Lanka and Maldives (on red list)
	ABTA said bookings were down 83% for summer 2021
August 2021	Cases continued to rise despite restrictions; a third wave of infections due to new Delta variant; a spike over 3 weeks as businesses reopened. People asked to return to working from home
	200 million people affected by COVID-19 by August 2021
September 2021	ONS coronavirus survey showed the highest number of deaths per 100,000 in Peru and other South American countries
	Surge in U.S. business travel demand (ADARA)
	U.K. CJRS scheme ended
December 2021	The U.K. government lifted restrictions to allow people to celebrate Christmas and New Year (not the response in other countries). No return to workplace in the United Kingdom
	Half of U.K. consumers shop online for nonfood products; 37% U.S. consumers do so

January 2022	Spike in infections, especially from the new Omicron variant—the highest rates of infection than in previous waves of the pandemic. No testing required if fully vaccinated when entering the United Kingdom
	Facebook usage "plateaued"; Facebook use by teenagers dropped dramatically
	ABTA reports increase in bookings for 2022 and 2023
February 2022	The United States had seen 78 million cases, over 900,000 deaths; India 42 million cases, 500,000 deaths; the United Kingdom 18 million cases, 158,318 deaths (the highest number of deaths in western Europe)
March 2022	All restrictions lifted by the U.K. government as seen to be entering endemic rather than pandemic phase
	The United States, the United Kingdom, and Japan still not on the "white" list for entry to European countries so visitors still need to complete Passenger Locator Form on entry

The Initial Impact on Tourism and Hospitality

The Office for National Statistics (ONS) presented an alarming picture when looking back at the impact of the pandemic in the first few months (ONS February 2021). They show that:

- Air passenger arrivals to the United Kingdom fell from 6,804,900 in February 2020 to 112,300 in April 2020, a fall of 98.3 percent. We soon got used to seeing pictures of deserted airport terminals around the world (Figure 2.1).
- Greater London had just 20 percent of rooms occupied in July 2020 compared with 90 percent in July 2019.
- Accommodation and travel agency businesses saw the sharpest decline in turnover, and employment in these industries fell by a fifth when compared with the year before.
- The biggest drop in employment across the sector was for those aged 25 to 34 working full-time, closely followed by the 16- to 24-year-old group working part-time, compared with the same peak holiday season in 2019.
- In April 2020, the number of people traveling via Eurotunnel was 91.3 percent lower than the same period in 2019.

Figure 2.1 Airport terminals deserted

Across food and hospitality businesses, new options such as drive-through and takeaways were being trialed, although this was not a realistic option for many. In America, Ann Hsing of Pasjoli and Dialogue restaurants in Los Angeles stated that "the food we do, we learned very quickly on the first day, is not very translatable to takeout" as they include an 18- to 22-course tasting menu.

At the same time, a well-known bar in New York, Amor y Amargo, closed as one of the smaller establishments that had limited ability to ride out long-term cash flow problems. This scenario was predicted by investment bank UBS as early as April 2020, believing that around 20 percent of independent eating places were likely to stay closed because it would be too difficult to get started again. There may be fewer mid-range restaurants that survive long-term closure due to lockdown requirements, although it is not clear whether this will be the picture for more high-end establishments.

The hospitality industry was following guidance, trying to reduce close contact for customers with tables set out two meters apart and separated with Perspex screens. In New York, they allowed park visitors to sit in set-out socially distanced circles. The confidence of travelers to book trips depended on two main criteria: having the COVID-19 vaccine, stated by 47 percent of those surveyed (Global Rescue), and the reopening of borders for 34 percent, closely followed by feeling secure that they could get home in an emergency. There was a tentative start with Denmark, Switzerland, Austria, and Germany planning "controlled" opening in the early part of 2020, with Portugal, France, and Netherlands planning to reopen in June 2020.

Despite the continuing risks from the virus, and indeed the number of deaths in different parts of the world, airlines were starting to open some routes and people had started to travel. As the countries willing to allow visitors to arrive increased, there were still restrictions in many of them. Some businesses were still closed, masks were obligatory, and there were still some places that required long quarantine periods on arrival, so this was not a return to any version of "normal."

By the end of the first year of the pandemic, people's perceptions of the threat from COVID-19 had been quite stable for a while, certainly since June 2020. The threat was seen as greater to "the country" than to the individual, although it is not clear how this was defined. Around a quarter of the population was concerned about the financial impact, and this view continued until February 2021 and by now, 20 percent said they were worried they would struggle to pay their bills in a month's time.

How the Pandemic Was Viewed in 2021

Go forward to Spring 2021 when things started to change, the most restrictive rules were relaxed, and people were allowed to travel further—see more details in Table 2.2. In Germany, for instance, they were allowed to travel to other European countries for a holiday/vacation. Previously closed, nonessential shops and services were now allowed to reopen. Hospitality businesses could take visitors and were expected to minimize the risks to guests while "not knowingly" accepting those in breach of existing travel restrictions. How they were supposed to deal with this issue was not clear.

In the United Kingdom, guidance for tourism and hospitality was produced, clearly intended to cover every eventuality though not necessarily practicable for the smallest businesses. There were more detailed guidelines to follow for those based in Wales, the United Kingdom:

Businesses should also consider, where appropriate:

- *Strengthening their policy on safe disposal of face coverings for staff and visitors;*
- *Introducing measures for staff and visitors, on arrival, such as taking temperature tests, asking people to sanitize their hands, and asking questions around whether they are displaying any symptoms;*
- *Considering the flow of guests/visitors and how to avoid any household mixing by keeping guests/visitors apart as they move around the premises throughout their visit/stay, with particular regard to enclosed public areas such as lifts, stairs, and corridors;*
- *Instructing guests/visitors to move through enclosed public areas as quickly as possible, and to avoid shouting or singing in such areas;*
- *Within accommodation, ensuring that guests keep the doors to their rooms closed at all times, apart from when entering and leaving;*
- *Staggering room service/laundry delivery and so on to rooms, to avoid guests opening doors and coming out at the same time;*
- *Reviewing their incident and emergency procedures to ensure they reflect the physical distancing principles as far as possible, including considering how to minimize household mixing when congregating in fire assembly areas.*

As you can see, the responsibility for controlling the virus at this level was shifted to the individual business. In addition, for food and drink businesses, it was to be table service only, with no customers ordering or standing at the counter in a bar or pub. As outdoor venues could also reopen now, these measures were intended to "help the hospitality sector recover after a difficult 12 months" (Drakeford).

There was growing concern that as many as one in three could have COVID-19 without showing any symptoms, so the free lateral flow tests became more widely available. The vaccination program started to spread rapidly across regions, and people then began to see the threat level for coronavirus fall. In some local areas, there were still concerns about the impact on personal finances and whether they could pay their bills after the next month. Wealthier areas did not feel the negative impact so much, of course, but those living in the lower wage, poorer parts of the world would inevitably feel the strain.

International travel was still difficult, with extra safeguards introduced, though not consistently across all regions. Different views emerged about how safe people felt when traveling depending on whether other travelers had produced a negative COVID-19 test result or had received the vaccine dose(s). There was mistrust about how good the testing facilities were and how confident they could actually be in a negative result. This is not the same as having the vaccine which prevented you from contracting the virus in the first place (though not 100 percent effective).

Even more difficult was the range of testing requirements before traveling home, with each country devising its own set of rules. Lack of cohesive approach meant you might need a PCR test within 72 hours of returning home, but no guidance on where to get it or how to get the results in time. Finding a test center in a foreign country, one that was open and able to get the results back to you in the time limit, was an added level of stress for all travelers and, in some cases, just impossible.

It was vital to show visitors that everything was being done to ensure they were safe on the journey and once they reached their destination. However, by the end of May, people were becoming worried by the number of visitors traveling across country/county borders from places with high rates of infection into those with much lower rates.

In the United States, consultancy firm Longwoods International stressed that local residents also needed to feel safe and to see that visitors followed the rules in their region. This was certainly an issue in the United Kingdom, for example, where press and TV news coverage showed crowds of tourists at popular holiday resorts, having traveled from COVID hotspots into Wales where stricter travel restrictions had been imposed for longer and rates of infection were low.

If you were working in tourism and hospitality, this presented even more of a dilemma trying to balance the need to keep your business going with the real danger of infection spread. The request for visitors to self-test before traveling, and every two days while they were there, was clearly unenforceable, especially as the government was putting the responsibility onto accommodation providers—again—to notify guests of the rules when booking. Further unenforceable guidance said that guests testing positive should then go back home by the most direct route, but not by public transport—a difficult option if they had arrived by train?

The ongoing survey by the Direct Marketing Association (DMA) in March 2021 showed a range of positive views for businesses going forward but full recovery was not likely in the short term. At the same time, the ONS Coronavirus Infection Survey (CIS) had been in place for a year, providing useful data for governments and business leaders. As you can see from Figures 2.2 to 2.4, there were striking differences between the numbers of deaths and death rates in different regions (John Hopkins University).

While the columns (Series 1 in each Chart) show the total number of deaths attributed to COVID-19 for each country, the line (Series 2 in each Chart) clearly shows the death rate per 100,000 during January 2020 to September 2021. This was a significant point in the spread of the pandemic as we now saw it as an ongoing situation rather than a short-term "inconvenience." The charts also emphasize how the impact differed across nations and the full extent of infections and death rates for the local population, in some cases lower numbers of deaths but much higher rates overall.

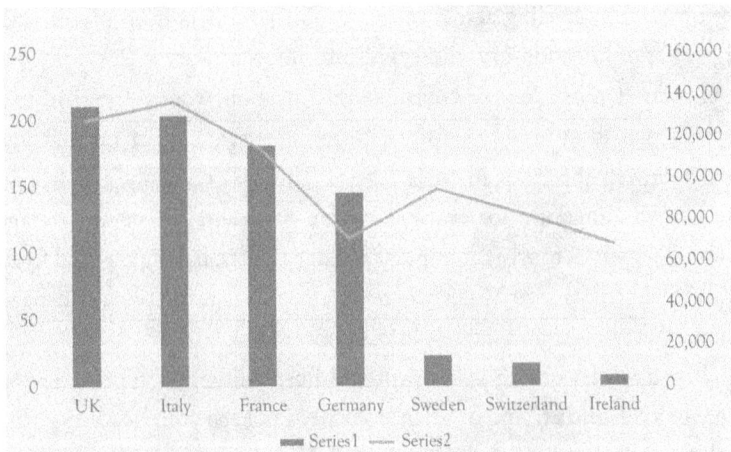

Figure 2.2 Global deaths and death rates Northern Europe

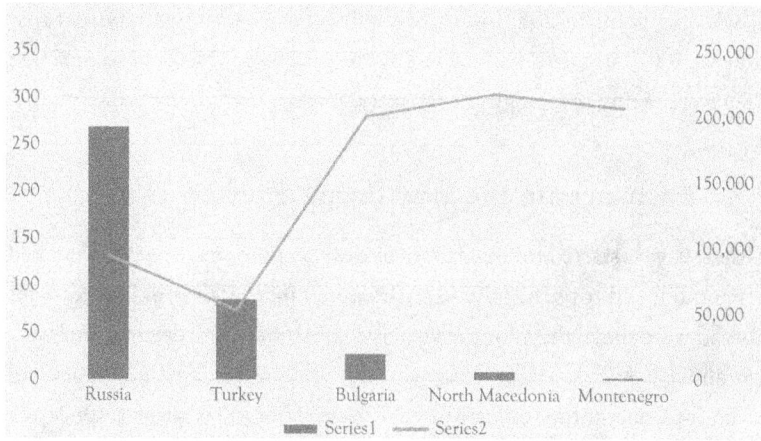

Figure 2.3 Global deaths and death rate Eastern Europe

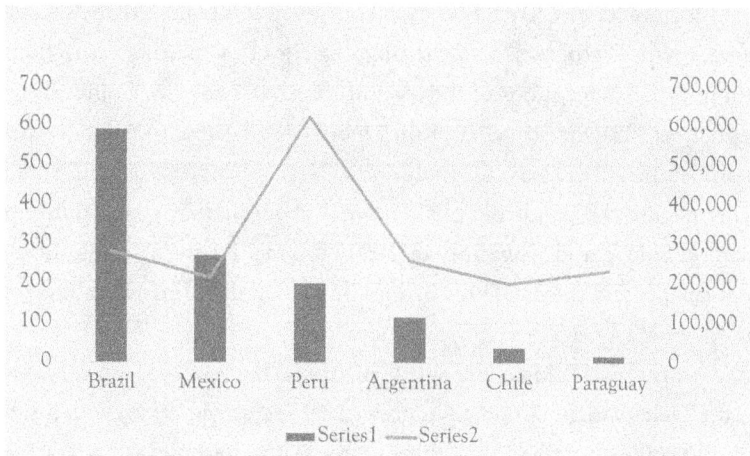

Figure 2.4 Global deaths and death rate South America

The alarming rate of deaths per 100,000 in Peru, and in some of the other countries in South America, showed how those countries with lower population numbers tended to have the worst outcomes once the virus reached them. Although there were high numbers of deaths reported in Brazil and Mexico, as well as Russia and Turkey in eastern Europe, for instance, the high population numbers mean that the overall death rate does not appear as extreme.

At this point in 2021, most of the businesses surveyed reported that they were still negatively impacted by the virus, though 63 percent stated they were seeing some signs of recovery.

Changes in the Way People Booked Trips

Other surveys started to see changes in the way potential travelers searched for and booked trips. In July, ADARA noted that U.K. bookings for trips abroad were the highest for the year as the "Amber List" destinations were announced. As this meant those who were fully vaccinated no longer had to go into quarantine on arrival back home, bookings surged. Once the announcement was made, bookings went up 23 percent in a day, were up 36 percent from the beginning of July, and were 65 percent higher than the month before.

The number of COVID-19 cases continued to rise despite the success of vaccination programs and the ongoing travel or meeting restrictions still in place. Perceptions of the level of threat was at a low point but by September, 25 percent believed they would not be able to pay bills in a month's time. There was still a substantial base of people struggling financially during the pandemic but note other sources that give a different picture. Solo Travel magazine, in 2021, found 71 percent of its survey participants said the pandemic had no impact on their financial ability to travel, with 14 percent saying they now had more funds available.

A third wave of infections was seen around August 2021, mainly due to the Delta variant (ONS). Numbers were increasing again, with a significant spike over a period of three weeks as businesses started to reopen and people were returning to the workplace. There was then another push for people to return to working from home if possible—confusing and conflicting guidance again over a brief period.

At the end of 2021, threats posed to the individual were believed to be quite low but, by now, there was growing concern that the threat to the country as a whole was greater than previously thought. With pressure from various industrial and political sources, there was a call to remove restrictions in the United Kingdom and allow people to celebrate Christmas and New Year. The government conceded even though the removal of all restrictions was not the response in other countries. As expected, given this short-term freedom, the number of infections and deaths continued to rise with the new Omicron variant rampant. However, the rates can be misleading as those who were infected were not as seriously ill as with the previous strains, and the high number of hospitalizations did not represent high rates in intensive care units (ICUs) as they had done previously.

CHAPTER 3

The Wider Impact of Restrictions During the Pandemic

Apart from the details listed previously, positive signs of how reduced travel had impacted the natural environment began to emerge. Travel restrictions meant that birds were returning to towns, skies appeared to be clearer with less smog or airborne particles, and air quality was much cleaner. Climate change was still an issue, and 76 percent of people surveyed in the United Kingdom said they had "concerns about global warming."

A key impact was that the reduction in carbon dioxide emissions, working remotely, and changes to travel plans had also meant people were walking or cycling more. Paris decided to establish "corona cycleways" and Milan introduced a system to prioritize pedestrians and cyclists in the city.

Travel Restrictions Introduced

The most obvious change was the introduction of travel restrictions for everyone. Cross-border travel stopped completely or at least was severely restricted to essential journeys only. This option was taken up by most countries around the world, with immediate cancellation of all modes of transport. This made life more difficult in countries where residents regularly traveled back and forth across county/region borders for work or shopping.

Images of fleets of planes at a standstill at major airports were shocking and news quickly spread of trains, boats, and coaches parked up indefinitely. Some journeys were still possible, but the issue of what constitutes "essential" became the major talking point.

For example, in some countries, essential journeys were classed as hospital/medical appointments and shopping. There were examples of armed police checking reasons for travel in towns where the strictest lockdown rules were imposed. There were also restrictions on distance you were allowed to travel from your home—five miles in some regions— although clearly this was not possible for those living in rural areas and, indeed, was unenforceable.

The other essential journey was for employment if you were classed as an essential or key worker. This was alongside the critical requirement for full lockdown. The guidance, soon to be law, was to work from your own home, if possible; only leave the house for essential trips; and no social mixing with other households. It became a very emotive subject, as we can see from the essential worker notice (Figure 3.1) that clearly shows there was some frustration with anyone not following the rules. Back to the issue of what counts as essential with confusing messages from different national governments.

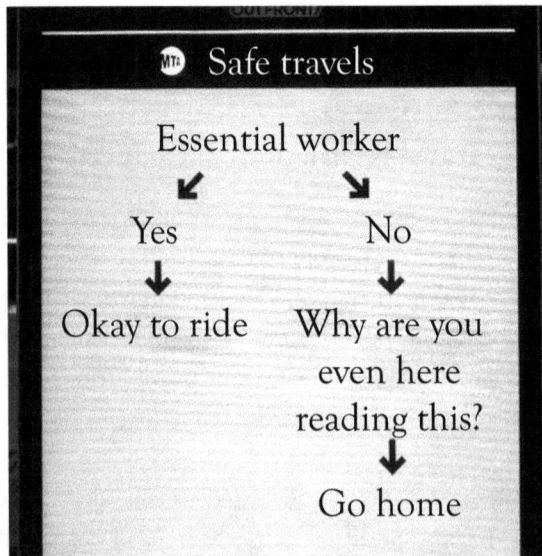

Figure 3.1 Safe Travels' essential worker notice

Remember that in early 2020, countries were trying to deal with a completely new and unknown global emergency. It quickly became obvious that this was a rapidly spreading, highly contagious form of virus completely impervious to geographic or political boundaries. Although figures were not necessarily accurate at that time, the immediate reaction, given the lack of any other effective means to halt the spread, was to stop people moving about. A virus doesn't move around, people do. So, a wide range of travel restrictions were introduced and the lockdown approach became the norm.

Shops, bars and restaurants, hotels, places of entertainment, schools, and nonessential places of work were closed with immediate effect. Images from around the world showed deserted major cities, such as Vienna (Figure 3.2) now eerily quiet with no pedestrians or traffic.

Confusion reigned! Essential shopping? Small independent stores were closed but larger retailers were allowed to stay open. Shelves were sealed off if deemed to be luxury goods. But, of course, lots of arguments about what counts as luxuries. There were arguments about babies' and children's clothes—what if there is a new-born baby or the kids really need a new pair of trousers as they just had a growth spurt of three inches?

Figure 3.2 Deserted city center streets: Vienna

Figure 3.3 Empty store shelves

Why were feminine hygiene products and some toiletries restricted but men's shaving essentials were not?

Until these issues were resolved, the first wave of lockdowns resulted in some fascinating choices by shoppers. Images from the United Kingdom quickly spread around the globe. Panic buying of essentials took on gigantic proportions with whole trolleys or carts full of toilet rolls. Really? Why? Supermarket/stores were stripped of basic foodstuff even though the stores urged people to shop normally as there was plenty of stock in their warehouses. Images of bewildered elderly shoppers looking at empty shelves were, indeed, shocking (Figure 3.3). Note this was not just experienced in the United Kingdom.

Decisions by governments changed rapidly as everyone tried to restrict the spread of the virus to safeguard their health services, and cope with soaring infection rates and deaths. Work began on trying to develop a vaccine as quickly as possible, but at this stage isolation was the major option to restrict the spread. Hindsight is great, but this was a completely new development that governments globally could not have foreseen.

Impact on Cruising

A major travel-related casualty of the pandemic from the beginning was the cruise ship sector. With an average age of 62 for world cruise passengers, compared with an average age of 47 across cruising in general, this presented additional issues for cruise companies to consider. From around 30 million cruise passengers in 2019 (cruisemummy.com), there were fewer than 6 million in 2020, the majority of passengers from North America. There were some positive signs of bouncing back for the industry by 2021 with nearly 14 million passengers. It took longer for cruises in the Mediterranean region to resume, with 95 percent fewer passengers in 2020 than in 2019 (cruisemummy.com)—a startling reduction to 255,000 passengers from nearly 4.5 million the year before.

It is even more revealing when you consider that there had been around 1.8 million people employed in the sector, and cruising generated over $154 billion to the global economy. In the United Kingdom, revenues for the cruise industry dropped by more than 70 percent, losses increasing daily as all cruises were suspended. Revenue and passenger numbers did recover a little once some form of cruising could continue with the focus on home waters around the British Isles (Statista 2021).

The larger cruise liners seemed to be the hardest hit as on-board infection rates increased at an alarming rate, among both passengers and staff, leading to complete isolation. Confined to their cabins for days, food delivered to their door, and no use of on-board facilities were not what the cruise holiday guests had planned.

Passengers and crew could not leave ships, and countries along their planned route refused to let them dock or disembark, so no onshore excursions were possible. For example, UAE, the Seychelles, and the Maldives banned all cruise ships and Canada banned ships with 500+ passengers until later in the summer.

There were many horror stories in the press, including 1,000 crew members stranded on a ship unable to get home, and one of the last cruise passengers finally arriving home to the United Kingdom from Australia on a now-deserted ship. Disaster from the customer's point of view, but the impact on the industry was devastating as they saw their cruise

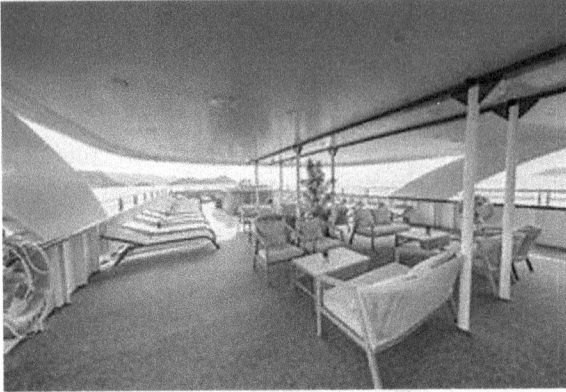

Figure 3.4 Deserted ships as cruises canceled

liners ready for customers but docked and completely deserted (as in Figure 3.4).

The Washington Post report (WP) highlighted two main questions about the cruise industry, which had basically stopped sailings from mid-March in 2020. What would cruising look like when it does get going again, and when is this likely to be? Major players in the industry made some statements about how they envisaged future cruise sailings, though at this stage the detailed plans were still under discussion.

Royal Caribbean Cruises expected to see shorter cruises, and both Carnival Cruise Line and Norwegian Cruise Line intended to use a limited number of their ships in the near future. Some of the smaller brands in cruising had tentative plans to start sailing again by the summer. Given the usual expectations of cruise passengers, it was unlikely that it would be the same once the sector restarts.

New guidance by CDCP said there must be "temperature checks, medical screenings, testing for the coronavirus, and social distancing protocols" on all cruise liners. Add the need to modify existing air filters, reduce capacity, and include stringent cleaning measures, this seems like a substantial change for the industry. What would now disappear from the usual offering to passengers? One of the things regularly mentioned was the removal of a help-yourself buffet counter, now only providing a serviced option for meals. With planned changes to itineraries, reduced numbers on shore excursions, and changes to entertainment on board, it may not seem such an attractive option as it did prepandemic.

Canceled Trips

As infection rates and deaths grew, countries took different actions to try and safeguard their nationals, although there were some countries that refused to acknowledge the pandemic potential during the early stages, including the United States and regions in South America.

If you were still determined to travel, everyone was advised to book a package that was ATOL protected rather than plan elements of a trip separately and to check in advance what restrictions applied at your destination. Thousands of trips were canceled at the last minute; the airline BA canceled flights to Milan as demand plummeted and stated that even postpandemic, they were pulling out of operating flights from Heathrow and Gatwick in England. They had lost 95 percent of flights from normal levels.

Grounded airlines included EasyJet, Virgin, and Ryanair, although Ryanair planned to restart 40 percent of flights in July and EasyJet by mid-June. By the end of April 2020, TUI had canceled all trips until the summer. Some countries were still open for visitors—such as France, Greece, and Bulgaria—despite restaurants, bars, and shops closed when you got there. Many of the major airlines were under attack for refusing to refund customers when their trips were canceled, even when their own regulations said they must do so.

Airlines were always going to endure the most travel restrictions of course. For example, Cathay Pacific said that lockdowns and the ban on transit traffic in Hong Kong had resulted in fewer than 500 passengers a day instead of the usual 100,000. Singapore Airlines recorded their first ever loss of £122 million and Ryanair a £178 million loss.

Among many airlines, there was anger that financial aid given to Lufthansa and Austrian Airlines was unfair, and Air France received bail-out funding on the condition they halved their carbon footprint by 2030. In the United Kingdom, BA threatened a legal challenge to the government arguing that the imposed 14-day quarantine requirement when returning from some countries was "irrational." To complete the picture, the aerospace industry was hit by plummeting demand for new, bigger planes.

How Passenger Actions Changed

A survey in April 2020 (ADARA) looked at the pattern for flight and hotel bookings in the United States. March was the point at which everything changed as everyone realized this was not a temporary inconvenience. Travel searches and bookings made at the same time dropped by 75 percent. Business flight bookings fell by 87 percent to a minimal level with leisure bookings following a similar pattern, down by 81 percent.

Demand for travel into the United States reduced as restrictions started to bite, with demand for travel 70 percent less than in 2019. People seemed to be a little more optimistic about traveling later in the year (though we know that didn't materialize) but it was too difficult to predict demand across different states.

The picture was similar in the United Kingdom (Schofield June 2020). IATA reported passenger demand was down by 94.3 percent from the year before and inbound visits from overseas residents was likely to fall around 60 percent by the end of the year. When asked, survey respondents said their biggest fear was uncertainty about financial stability of travel companies, and many also confirmed they would not travel overseas again until a vaccine was widely available.

It is interesting to look back at different research studies and see how, despite the massive fall in demand, there was still some optimism that it would be better by the end of the year.

However, there remained a strong lack of confidence in the travel industry and a reluctance to commit to booking an overseas trip. While domestic travel had been growing steadily in many countries worldwide up until the beginning of the pandemic, we now see a rapid increase in demand for accommodation where the visitors are in control of their environment—a significant increase in demand for self-catering facilities in less popular tourist destinations. In 2021, the staycation was now the option people were searching for but see later chapters on the impact of this change and whether it was good or bad for the sector.

CHAPTER 4

The Impact on People

As the spread of COVID-19 grew, the elderly were soon identified as the most vulnerable to the virus and more likely to suffer severe damage to their health, especially if they already had some form of underlying medical condition. Advice and guidance said they must stay isolated from everyone else, including family, stay indoors, and let others deliver their essential shopping. Added to this heart-breaking scenario, no contact allowed with older relatives in nursing facilities, sometimes during their final days, meant it was a desperate time for families around the world.

Some of the hardest hit groups during the early lockdowns and restrictions were those with major celebration/family events planned. Weddings, which we know take a long time to plan, were suddenly canceled by venues with no prospect of a future date to rebook. Celebratory events for birthdays and anniversaries, baptisms, and important dates in the religious calendar were canceled at short notice. Arguments about cash or voucher refunds, or booking for a new date in the future, took over the headlines.

Working From Home

A major element of change was the guidance/pressure to work from home if possible. Sounds like a useful solution if you are office based, and there were suggestions that up to 50 percent of usual business travel would be lost permanently (Ben Baldanza). However, in practice, this presented further problems. There are positives associated with working from a home base rather than a central place of work, including:

- Less time and money spent on travel and commuting to the workplace;
- More time with the family and less need for childcare provision, although this might be a negative result in some cases;

- Potentially less time spent socializing with work colleagues;
- Easier to focus on work projects with fewer distractions.

There are also negatives associated with a change to homeworking, such as:

- The need to be motivated and organized to focus on work tasks;
- More family interruptions likely, especially if there are small children to care for and you have to keep them happy too (as in Figure 4.1);
- The need for access to consistent, excellent quality Internet connections: this became an issue depending on what region you lived in;
- Problems with children and parents/carers working from the same home and difficulties in accommodating everyone's need to use the IT broadband facilities at the same time.

Homeworking was less common among younger age groups (up to 24 years old). This could reflect the type of industry they worked in, such as hospitality, entertainment, or recreation, where homeworking was not a workable option so they were more likely to be on the furlough scheme (ONS).

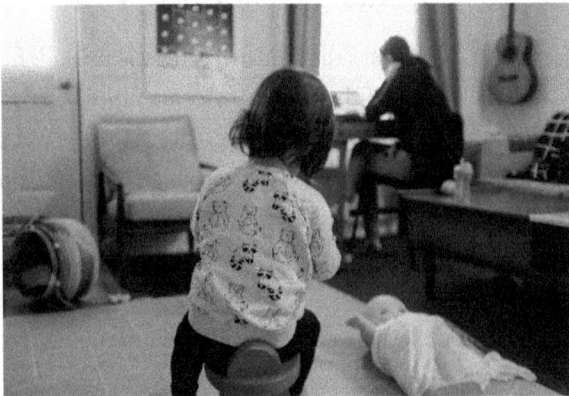

Figure 4.1 Homeworking with a small child

This requirement found 60 percent of the U.K. population working from home and 83 percent of employees in a survey for an insurance provider saying they did not need an office to be productive (Schofield). The development of this theme is that it is more appropriate to refer to it as remote working, and people can be more creative about how they see their workspace in any location.

Both vacation rental company Vrbo and home rental company Airbnb had already seen a trend starting to emerge, with 40 percent of Airbnb bookings early in the pandemic being long-term stays. If you are working remotely from a base, then why not a very attractive vacation spot? For Airbnb, this meant they started to offer long-term monthly rentals, and they see this as a "profound shift" in rentals globally. After all, it is much more relaxing staying in a home with all the facilities than in a hotel room.

To support this approach, both companies required new cleaning procedures to be followed by hosts to reassure visitors that they will be as safe as possible from infection and to encourage them to travel again. We see later that the issue of cleanliness at the location, as well as on the journey, is at the top of the list when travelers are deciding to book a trip. The traditional star rating for cleanliness is now more important than ever.

Homeworking has, therefore, been a significant feature of the pandemic, with mixed reactions from businesses and workers who were now required to use their own home as a workstation. By the autumn of 2021, Malcolm Bell, chief executive of Visit Cornwall, cautioned that for those working from home, "home" was no longer a sanctuary and people had had enough of being stuck within the same four walls. On a more positive note, he also suggested that the flexibility of working away from a central office location meant they were, perhaps, likely to take more frequent, shorter, holiday/vacation breaks. And we have already seen that you can interpret homeworking as working remotely so, why not choose to complete the work schedule in a different location? Much more relaxing as we can see (Figure 4.2).

Overall, there is evidence from various sources suggesting that working away from a central company base had been effective for most businesses and workers did manage to achieve work targets set for them. By the end of 2021, the United Kingdom had shown no sign of a complete

Figure 4.2 Relaxed remote working

return to the workplace full time (ONS). The preferred option appears to be a mix between two and three days a week working from home, with 37.5 percent of millennials wanting to work away from the central office between two and four days a week.

The conclusion drawn is that given this picture, business travel to and from a place of work is unlikely to bounce back to prepandemic levels. In addition, people either have a backlog of annual leave still to take with limited options for somewhere to go, or redundancies and reduced pay mean they can no longer think about planning holidays/vacations abroad.

Clearly there was a major impact on travel as the numbers dropped dramatically, particularly on public transport. Traffic into major urban and city areas consisted of key workers and those for whom working from home was not feasible, with many scheduled transport services reduced. On the other hand, online ordering of essential and other goods rocketed leading to an increase in delivery vehicle traffic.

Anyone who was unable to work from home, but was not counted as an essential key worker, was likely to be put on some form of furlough scheme, which involved being paid to stay at home.

Education was hit extremely hard with schools, colleges, and universities in many countries closed and "home schooling" the buzz words. Popular with some, not so popular with others! School-related travel was

Figure 4.3 Normally busy motorways/freeways were empty

now curtailed, including private vehicles of parents and teachers, school bus, and public transport services. Roads were eerily quiet, especially motorways/freeways that were usually crammed with commuter traffic (Figure 4.3).

A particularly negative result from major businesses and corporations closing, or reducing the workforce at, a central workplace was the almost total lack of footfall for small independent stores, cafes, or restaurants. These were some of the first to see their customer base disappear. While many governments introduced schemes to provide some form of financial help, this would never be enough long term.

In the United Kingdom, a furlough scheme was introduced to help pay staff wages, up to 80 percent of their normal pay with the employer topping up the remaining 20 percent so reducing their payroll bill. Some county or local authority fees were frozen for a while to try and ease cash flow problems, but by 2021, many of these independent businesses had been forced to close.

In some cases, the changes led to innovative approaches to reaching and serving a new customer base, but this did depend on the type of business or industry sector you were in.

Social Inequalities Emerged

Many political leaders (Members of Parliament in the United Kingdom) stated at the time that "COVID-19 thrives on inequalities" and this became more obvious as the pandemic continued, with every country seeing the poorest sectors of their population hardest hit by the virus and its wider impact.

As the travel restrictions and lockdown took hold globally, the social inequalities started to become more prominent. Lockdown meant staying at home except for appointments, essential shopping, and exercise. While it was difficult for everyone, it was extremely hard for those already living in the poorest areas with crowded inadequate facilities, often in high-rise flats, apartments, or temporary accommodation and without a safe garden or outdoor area for exercise. There were large numbers of households with poor or no Internet access, several children now at home instead of at school, and limited income to pay for the inevitable increases in cost of utilities—having the heating on all day, for instance.

If members of the family were also put on lower wages or a furlough scheme, and now forced to stay at home instead of work, frustration soon set in. It is difficult to keep children occupied if they have to stay at home for any reason, but having to keep isolated from friends and family indoors, just able to look through a window or door (as in Figure 4.4),

Figure 4.4 Children in isolation at home

had a significant impact on their well-being as lockdown requirements continued. While crime rates in some regions reduced overall by around 25 percent, rates of domestic violence went up sharply as people were forced to stay at home, frustrated, struggling to cope in what may have already been a tense environment. No options for escape.

At the same time, there were some good-news, positive reactions as community help groups were set up as well as food or clothing banks. This still meant loneliness and isolation were widespread among the elderly, young single parents without their normal support groups, and those who lived alone.

All medical and hospital facilities were focused on treating those affected by the virus, resulting in many other support facilities being closed. Although it was not a considerable proportion of travel at the time, opportunities for vacations specializing in tourists with physical disabilities, or specific medical conditions, had been a growing feature at the beginning of the pandemic (JJ/STA).

It was a huge disappointment for them and their carers, adding to the ever-growing number of groups who were struggling with their health and well-being. University and college students were not able to get home to stay with parents but were isolated in their term-time accommodation, with no face-to-face tuition, and for foreign students it became even harder as they could not fly home to family. Not being able to travel and visit elderly or vulnerable family members affected all age or social groups.

There was great relief when the first lockdowns finished, but by the second enforced lockdowns that took place later in the year and into 2021 across most of the world, the situation worsened. Not being able to travel far during a warm, summer season is not the same as being restricted during a cold, miserable winter! Yet the pandemic continued to spread despite every effort.

CHAPTER 5

Tourism and Travel— What Changed?

There was a complete breakdown of tourism and hospitality sectors with a dramatic, immediate, effect. As we have seen, the travel industry was the hardest hit with air travel virtually stopped and airports deserted. Public transport to and from airports was minimal, around 20 percent of normal capacity, with the emphasis on serving key workers. By the middle of 2020, those going back to work in the United Kingdom were told to expect only 10 percent of usual travel provision, and around the world trains were canceled and rail stations deserted—Figure 5.1 of an empty rail station in Australia became the norm. Not an encouraging sign for anyone.

Leisure Travel

Travel and tourism are a major source of revenue globally and, in some countries, the biggest contributor to GDP. At the beginning of the pandemic, the general situation regarding leisure travel was based around the following choices by customers (JJ):

- The planning stage was critical, around six months in advance for more mature travelers rather than last-minute or impulse purchases more likely from younger age groups.
- There was a feeling that people did not recognize themselves in advertising literature. User-generated images (UGIs) rather than the company's own images (even though these might be better quality) were growing in importance as an incentive to book.

Figure 5.1 Empty rail stations and canceled trains

- Social media marketing was vital but use of different plat-forms was noticeably dependent on age group. At this time, e-mail and Facebook were more popular for 50+ age groups with WhatsApp/TikTok and Instagram used more by Genera-tion Z and millennials.
- Overtourism was becoming a critical issue globally, the most popular tourist destinations overcrowded and suffering struc-tural and environmental damage from increased footfall.
- The Bucket List was recognized across all age groups although there were signs that the content was starting to change.
- The environmental impact, and recognition of the need to reduce carbon footprint, was increasingly an element of where people wanted to visit and how they got there. Tour operators and everyone involved in hospitality sectors saw this as an issue they must consider, so changes to how they promoted tourism had started to filter through.
- For the more mature travelers, there was increasing interest in finding new and exciting destinations to visit and the adven-ture "gap year" was suddenly looking attractive.

At this time, the USTA believed that despite problems for the sector, leisure travel would be the first to bounce back, although this was likely to be for shorter regional trips than further afield. With leisure travel severely reduced, trips canceled, and no new bookings feasible, given the uncertain future, a follow-up survey in 2021 showed a much more somber picture with little enthusiasm to plan ahead.

Hotels

For leisure travel, hotels had to think quickly about how to help potential visitors feel safe enough to make a booking. In particular, they had to ensure guests would see how important their well-being was, and this was their priority. Guidance appeared from several sources, including Frank Lavey from Hyatt hotels saying that they had listened to what guests said were their main concerns, so "health and safety is a top priority" (WP).

At the same time, the American Hotel and Lodging Association recommended that direct contact with guests should be reduced through greater use of technology. For instance, they suggested online booking, contactless payment systems, and restricting numbers of guests in lobby areas.

These measures are a concern, though, for anyone working in the hotel industry. The point about staying as a guest is that you want to feel welcome, feel comfortable, but keeping the staff at a distance takes away that feeling of "hospitality" the brochure promised originally. If the lobby area is no longer the comfy lounge area for meeting up with friends, it no longer feels like a leisure break.

There is no doubt that guests would expect to see more obvious cleaning activities around the hotel, likely to include all floor staff throughout the day as in Figure 5.2, with hand sanitizers and transparent shields in place at the service desks, all reminders of the ever-present virus. If the hotel also starts to remove things like mini-bar goods and menus and insists on prebooking individual times to use the gym or other facilities, the element of a relaxing stay is removed. After all, you do not want to feel like you are "entering a hospital" (Kate Walsh, Cornell University School of Hotel Administration). So, a difficult balance for hotels to achieve as they start to welcome guests again.

Figure 5.2 Ensuring hotel areas are regularly cleaned

Business Travel

What of business travel which is generally a major source of revenue? The following list summarizes the situation as it was at the beginning of the pandemic.

- Major cities around the world saw increasing volumes of regular commuter traffic, at specific periods each day, causing massive overcrowding on public transport.
- Vehicle usage continued to rise, causing traffic hold-ups and long tailbacks which meant growing levels of toxic emissions.
- Time restrictions were being introduced in major cities for delivery vehicles, an attempt to reduce congestion and bottlenecks.
- There was conflicting guidance on the use of diesel/petrol/gas and prices changing rapidly for customers (though not necessarily reflecting changes in oil prices worldwide). This was becoming more of an issue for larger commercial vehicles.
- Electric-powered vehicles were being developed alongside other fuel sources.
- Cycle lanes and pedestrianized areas were being introduced or extended, again impacting on delivery vehicles in particular.

- Face-to-face meetings were the norm, staff often traveling long distances cross-country or across borders, to attend a 2- to 3-hour meeting
- Large-scale international conferences and exhibitions around the world meant that delegates and speakers, with their display stand staff, represented the bulk of travelers and users of hospitality facilities around that location.
- Some airlines were associated more with business travel rather than the leisure market. For example, budget airlines focused on holidaymakers visiting traditional vacation destinations, with others catering for business travelers by offering a more comfortable experience where price is not a priority.
- Business travel flight bookings were more likely to be last-minute bookings where convenience and route are the major factors in the decision. Also note that at that time, evidence suggested that loyalty programs did not take preference in the decision making (JJ).

We reflect on some of these issues in more detail later, but it is a useful starting point to see how much things changed over more than two years of restrictions. As we can see from the surveys about when businesses expected staff to travel again, Figure 5.3 shows there was still an optimistic view of how soon this would resume.

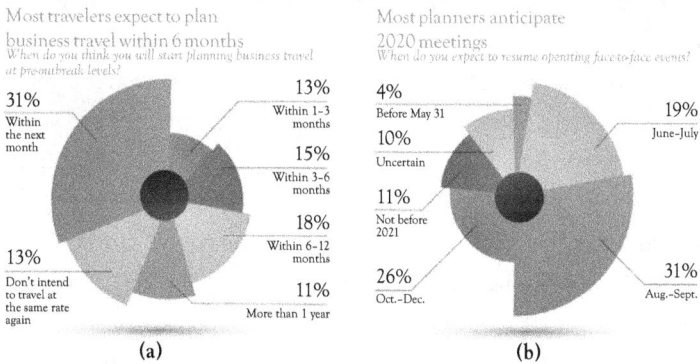

Most travelers expect to plan business travel within 6 months
When do you think you will start planning business travel at pre-outbreak levels?

- 31% Within the next month
- 13% Within 1-3 months
- 15% Within 3-6 months
- 18% Within 6-12 months
- 11% More than 1 year
- 13% Don't intend to travel at the same rate again

(a)

Most planners anticipate 2020 meetings
When do you expect to resume operating face-to-face events?

- 4% Before May 31
- 10% Uncertain
- 11% Not before 2021
- 26% Oct.-Dec.
- 19% June-July
- 31% Aug.-Sept.

(b)

Figure 5.3 *When do you intend to start traveling again?*

Source (a): Magid April 7-10 survey of 1,000 U.S. travellers; results weighted by age, gender, ethnicity, and region.
Source (b): I-Meet April 13-20 survey of more than 900 meeting planners worldwide.

Some business travel did continue during this period but at much lower rates as companies started to consider how necessary these trips were. At the beginning of the pandemic, business travel may not have been the biggest volume of sales for flights and rail, but it certainly represented the major source of income.

Timing and convenience were often the primary concerns for organizations rather than cost. While these are still crucial, of course, the cessation of travel during 2020–2021 has forced companies to rethink how often staff need to travel and, indeed, the wider impact on the environment of how and when they do so. It might also mean that what used to be a regular weekly meeting with a client now changes to a visit only when necessary.

Unless a business is purely online, with no need for contact with a customer or supplier, there is still a potential need to meet up with clients or suppliers at some stage in the process. This might be to procure goods, to generate new sales, or to maintain a cooperative relationship. For example, staff involved with sales need to make sure a new client sees at least a sample of a product and ensure correct dimensions or quantities are ordered. We all know of someone who has ordered goods online only to find they are very different from the images and descriptions on a website!

Once ordered, online goods have to be delivered to customers (individuals, manufacturers, retail outlets) and there may also be returned goods to collect and take back. Increased ordering online means increased road traffic at the point of delivery as well as increased rail and air freight transport to local drop-off points. Many countries/states have introduced measures to restrict access to busy urban areas for large-scale road vehicles, with time restrictions for delivery vehicles introduced in an attempt to reduce congestion and bottlenecks. Add the increasing volumes of regular commuter traffic, at specific periods each day and causing massive overcrowding on public transport, even without a pandemic, and some of these options would have to change.

Face-to-face meetings were the norm, staff traveling long distances cross-country or across borders to attend a two- or three-hour meeting. Staff meetings are often seen as wasting more time than is warranted by the outcomes. If you include transport to and from the meeting, plus any overnight stays for some staff, it does suggest it is an inefficient, very costly, way to keep people informed. On the other hand, it is also recognized that there are advantages for the company and staff members if they have a chance to meet up with others face-to-face occasionally.

The way people travel for business is an ongoing issue. The study for USA Today (USA Today) compared the time, and cost, of traveling by rail or air between points A and B on the most popular business flight routes. The train is considerably cheaper and the timescale, once you include waiting time at airports, is not hugely different. Rail travel also means working on administration stuff can be easier throughout the journey— no phones on flight mode for instance.

Realistically, it is accepted that a flight is a better use of time over longer distances and across borders, and the cost or environmental impact may be lower down the list of booking criteria. It is a balancing act for the business, especially when you consider that the biggest part of most corporate travel spend is for food and other expenses rather than flights. While company policy may be clear on what and how travel should be arranged, evidence suggests it is not necessarily clear to the staff involved, especially if they need to arrange bookings themselves.

Conferences and Exhibitions

Conferences and exhibitions are sometimes seen as a subset of the travel industry (ONS) with different patterns of activity from those referred to as leisure or business. This is a crucial element of the marketing strategy, for all sorts of products or services, and choosing this option has steadily increased globally. They involve several nights' stay and long distances from the company location, large numbers of visitors in their thousands, as well as large venues to cater for exhibitors. This means large-scale events represent the bulk of travelers and users of hospitality facilities around that location. While it does give companies a chance to reach a much wider audience over a shorter space of time, all of them already interested in the product or services featured, transporting staff and stands inevitably adds to costs.

The pandemic changed everything for the events management sectors, representing a "revolution" seen as either a catalyst or catastrophe

(EM blog). Event planning professionals had to fundamentally change and adapt to a new reality. For instance, in the United Kingdom, 90 percent of event professionals had seen some, if not all, of their business gone within a year.

At this time, 30 percent of event planners said they would never attend in-person meetings under any circumstances, given the pandemic, and around another third would only attend small local events. Only 14 percent of these professionals said they had no concerns about attending.

Just over half of them said safety was the number one issue for planners and also the biggest obstacle, with the vaccine roll-out being the biggest game changer (remember this was before the vaccine program was really in full swing globally). A quarter of them forecast that by the middle of 2021, in-person events would be taking place again and around a third believed it would be closer to the end of the year.

Respondents to the autumn survey for the Event Manager blog in 2020 (Event MB) thought that small and simple meetings will be the most common (21 percent), followed by in-house meetings (18 percent). This was echoed by Julius Solaris, editor of Event MB, which provides information on meetings and events. He believed that events would be local rather than national or international, much shorter over a day rather than several days, and with each session of the day only around 30 minutes. If you must keep people at a distance from each other, then smaller audiences have to be catered for. This was the only way he could see events taking place in the next year or so, accepting that a hybrid option mixing in-person and virtual attendance as the other alternative. It was widely accepted that traditional large-scale conferences, trade shows, and other events could not continue with these new conditions included.

It is expected that mid-tier hotels and meeting spaces will continue to be the first choice for 37 percent of event organizers, but it was seen that top-tier spaces may increase in popularity as they often have bigger outdoor areas to accommodate delegates (to take care of social distancing requirements and safety). Demand for these locations is likely to increase in 2022 and beyond, with prices rising as properties need to recoup previous losses.

The majority of respondents in this study thought that budgets, as well as cost per attendee, would decrease in 2021. There were some interesting thoughts on what organizers would do if budgets decreased, with off-site optional activities likely to be the first to go. If budgets increased, they would use any extra funds for increased technology equipment and facilities. From an investment viewpoint, other studies found 40 percent of marketing professionals planning to increase investment into virtual conferences and webinars as they went forward into 2022 (HubSpot) plus nearly the same number planning to spend the same.

The virtual option for attendees is sure to stay into 2022 and beyond. A good example of a small hybrid event (event manager blog) took place in Australia where they had 25 attendees in person and 25 virtual attendees. Food packs were given to those who could attend in person and personalized, branded food packs were delivered to the virtual attendees beforehand; 95 percent of delegates gave positive feedback of "very good" or "excellent."

Another event, the MRO Americas conference for aviation industries, is usually held in Orlando. It saw 8,000 attendees in person in 2019, but this number had broken down evenly into 4,000 in person and 4,000 virtual attendees by 2020 (Ben Baldanza). At the time, everyone was dealing with constant changes to regulations and restrictions because of COVID-19, so this was an impressive number of attendees in person. So, if the customer is looking to attend an event in person, there has to be added value somewhere—see some of the later discussions about hybrid events.

Microsoft also holds its annual "Ignite" event in Orlando, catering for more than 27,000 attendees in 2019. The same event in 2021, presented in a virtual format, hosted 270,000 attendees. Bob Bejan from Microsoft's Global Events team believes this has always been a likely scenario, but the pandemic has accelerated it into a primary role for all businesses (WP).

Experience of hosting virtual or hybrid events during the pandemic has brought out the benefits for business, accepting that it was the only option for a while. We will look at these later, but the key benefits include:

- Keep the costs of the conference venue down (there will still need to be some form of central venue to operate from).
- Keep the cost down for people wanting to attend so increasing the likely pool of attendees who sign up.

- Allow for higher numbers to take part and interact with others across country and regional borders without the costs to them of travel and accommodation.
- Create a recording of events that can be used as an extra product in the future.

It became evident that a Duty of Care was seen as a primary element in planning a conference or trade show, with disinfection and social distancing protocols crucial. USTA (2021) felt that it is easier to ensure such safety protocols at large-scale business gatherings than in some other environments. These health and safety protocols must also be followed by the supporting ground transport vehicles. There were some interesting points made about how ground transport is often the element that attendees are not happy with. After all, attendees must be happy and willing to travel, though that is more likely to be closer to home now than internationally.

The Key Travel Demographic 2021 (ITIJ) found 85 percent of American workers see in-person events as "irreplaceable" and a staggering 81 percent said they miss these meetings most of all. The report by Trondent in 2021 (Trondent travel report) also found that around 70 percent of business travelers agreed it was difficult to build up a real relationship with a client online, even more of them (91 percent) saying they would rather close a deal in person. With such views, it is difficult to see the projected rates of reductions in business travel being possible.

In June 2021, USTA suggested that business travel was not likely to recover until at least 2024, so a sobering thought to keep in mind. They quote business travel spending down 76 percent since the pandemic, equaling $97 billion loss. Things changed during the latter half of 2021 (ADARA) when, after lots of "dramatic dips and spikes," there had been a surge in demand by U.S. business travelers.

It is clear that we will continue to see a digital, virtual offering to participants as the norm in the future. There are other events that cannot easily be changed to a virtual format. Large-scale gatherings, even as outdoor events, have been seriously affected by the pandemic. As social distancing rules have changed, sometimes across neighboring states or counties, it has been impossible to change the format of festivals or parades which rely on people actually getting together. For the businesses that organize them, sell tickets, or use them to raise funds, the only option has been to cancel them. As the CEO of the International Festivals and Events Association says (IFEA), you cannot do temperature checks and keep everyone socially distanced along a parade route!

The American Express Global Business Travel forecast mentioned in the report (Ben Baldanza) includes some critical observations, including that "Meetings have to happen." It provides some interesting reflections on business travel globally, reinforcing the view that there is clear evidence of how global organizations have "transitioned from in-person to virtual events." I particularly love the comments about assumptions that all attendees are the same, that everyone loves the opening reception and networking until midnight or that they are comfortable being on camera. In his blog, Gerardo Tejado stresses that there is a need for a more individualized approach in the future to reflect these differences.

It is important to make the most of technology, especially as it will be "a few years before air fares and hotel rates become stable and predictable." This report also reiterates the point that there needs to be more scrutiny into business travel overall, whether a meeting needs to happen, and greater focus in policies to reflect employee safety.

A further report by American Express goes on to state that "business travel is needed to re-energise the global economy." At the time of publication, their forecast notes that rapid predeparture COVID testing was needed instead of quarantine, particularly for a London–New York corridor, a valid point at the time although such restrictions are no longer an issue in 2022.

It is recognized that streaming events digitally had led to a reduction in climate pollution by 60 to 98 percent. Based on this, two-thirds of respondents said they will use a hybrid format once the in-person events resume. After the initial shock of global shutdowns/postponements/cancellations, the industry is now adjusting, but basically people still want to meet face-to-face. In their feature on 6 Ways COVID-19 Will Change Travel in 2021—Expert Predictions (Hello! 2021) the authors suggested that there is "no replacement for in-person meetings" as people were suffering from "Zoom fatigue" and just wanted to meet up again.

During the earlier stages of the pandemic, event professionals were asked about their plans to travel "when the outbreak ends," as shown in Figure 5.4. Clearly this was when everyone was still convinced it would be fairly short-lived and they were reviewing how their particular work

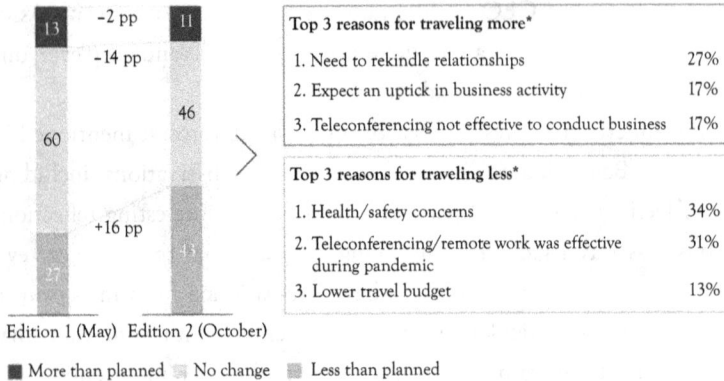

Top 3 reasons for traveling more*	
1. Need to rekindle relationships	27%
2. Expect an uptick in business activity	17%
3. Teleconferencing not effective to conduct business	17%

Top 3 reasons for traveling less*	
1. Health/safety concerns	34%
2. Teleconferencing/remote work was effective during pandemic	31%
3. Lower travel budget	13%

Edition 1 (May) Edition 2 (October)

■ More than planned   No change   Less than planned

Figure 5.4 Plans to travel in the next two years

environment had changed. After two years of a global pandemic, the view is that it will never "end" but will go from pandemic status to endemic status so we will have to find ways to live with it.

Noting that the U.K. events industry is worth £70 billion, and 50 percent of that is visitor spend, you cannot get that from virtual meetings. As a result of their experience during the first year of the pandemic, more than half of event planning professionals said they would address sustainability in their 2021 plans. Despite the continuing restrictions following these initial surveys, and the need to push back their original plans to 2022–2023, we can now see the importance of sustainability as a growing element of future events planning.

CHAPTER 6

Was It All Bad for the Travel and Tourism Sector?

There is evidence that attitudes toward the commute and business travel had started to change before the pandemic. Depending on the geographic location and available transport links, staff had increasingly been prepared to travel longer distances for work, particularly when housing prices have risen around major cities. While older staff members start to find travel less enjoyable than it used to be, there is evidence to suggest that younger millennials tend to enjoy the opportunity to travel for business, especially if it includes stopovers or a chance to combine it with some leisure time.

The Airlines

As we know, some airlines have always been associated with corporate business travel rather than the leisure market. For example, budget airlines focused on holidaymakers visiting traditional vacation destinations, with others catering for business travelers by offering a more comfortable experience where price is not a priority. Note there are some that also support small and medium size businesses, where price is more likely to be an important consideration, by offering something more in line with the leisure market. In addition, business travel flight bookings were more likely to be last-minute bookings where convenience and route are the major factors in the final decision. Also note that at that time, evidence suggested that loyalty programs did not always take preference in the decision-making process, certainly not for around a fifth of millennials who said it was not of interest (Trondent/JJ).

The Business Travel Association noted that business travelers represent around 15 to 20 percent of airline customers and are often more profitable than leisure customers. But travel management companies had lost 90 percent of revenue since 2019, with business travelers also having the biggest negative impact on city destinations.

As the trend grows for companies to rely less on face-to-face meetings and more on technology for communication between workers, it is likely that corporate travel numbers will be slower to show any increase. However, airlines have continued to operate during the pandemic, albeit at much reduced numbers and across restricted routes, so it is interesting to consider whether they can continue to operate in the same way as we come out of the most limiting restrictions.

In order to keep going, airlines may have blocked off seats or limited how many tickets are sold. While the pandemic has instilled the notion of social distancing into everyday life for us all, it is inevitable that we will have to sit next to someone we do not know the next time we fly. The CEO of JetBlue emphasized that airlines have to cover costs, and to break-even this is usually 75 to 80 percent capacity. Operating at less than this, as they have done during 2020–2021, is unsustainable especially as demand starts to go up again.

Changes that were introduced to keep going during the pandemic are likely to stay in place afterwards. We have seen changes that were quickly introduced, such as restricted food services on flights, wearing a mask throughout the journey, and, in some cases, extra health questionnaires to complete. Guidance from the International Civil Aviation Organization (ICAO) also suggested restricting access to toilet facilities (not completely sure how this works in practice on longer journeys) and carry-on luggage to be stored underneath the seat rather than overhead.

International travel was becoming more accessible as prices started to reduce at the start of the pandemic, but any further decreases to get passengers moving again as we come out of the biggest restrictions are likely to be short-lived, for both flights and hotels. If fewer people travel, then the costs for all elements of international travel will go up thus making it more expensive for everyone. As Rick Steves (European travel expert from the United States) says, he can afford to cover these price hikes but others cannot. Basically, there is a real danger that international travel will only be possible for the wealthiest people.

The Negative Impact of Safe Travel Lists

During 2020–2021, given the mix of responses globally as countries decided which inbound/outbound travel was allowed, different systems were introduced, including a traffic light system depending on how high infection and death rates were in the destination. This also led to restrictions being lifted or reduced after a spike in infections and death rates. Airlines such as BA were encouraging governments to allow tourists to travel in order to get the economy moving again.

Popular European destinations were planning to open again, including Italy, Spain, Germany, and Croatia, as their economies relied heavily on tourism spend. But the issue of quarantine remained unresolved with no agreement between countries. Note that during the first year of restrictions, many hospitality facilities were still closed to visitors even if they could actually get there.

The major block to booking a holiday/vacation for British passengers was this traffic light system. It was meant to be the easy-to-understand grading system for judging safety of destinations but turned out to be a disaster. Two-thirds of potential travelers blamed it for putting them off going overseas. There was a constant stream of scathing comments in the press, and in various industry surveys, about the confusing and "ill thought-out decisions" by the British government. However, 20 percent stated that they had taken a holiday abroad despite the restrictions and government advice not to travel unless absolutely necessary.

We have seen booking habits change consistently as governments amended the destination "safe list." Every time a country was added to Green (safe) or Amber (OK at the moment) status, there was a significant spike in bookings. For example, Malta and Croatia saw more than 40 percent rise in bookings in July 2021. A trend also highlighted by ADARA (UK Summer Insights 2021) was that countries already on the Green list at the time seemed to lose out to the new ones added. However, note many of these were long-haul destinations, so reflecting other signs that people were choosing to book shorter journeys.

There were similar spikes in bookings for countries added to the Amber list, some seeing more than 20 percent increase when the change of status was announced. It is an interesting reflection on the success of the traffic light system when there were surges in bookings for Red list countries at the time despite the stricter quarantine rules. For instance, bookings for Sri Lanka rose by 25 percent and the Maldives by a third.

Across the world, blame for the chaos about travel and taking holidays/vacations outside the home country was firmly placed on the U.K. government, while the travel industry itself had the public's sympathy (but was not seen as totally blameless).

Reintroducing Restrictions

As infection rates spiked again globally, it was clear that restrictions needed to be reimposed in order to stop the spread of the virus. So, throughout 2021, we saw fluctuating demand for travel with no consistency from either travel companies or the individual traveler.

We have seen travel-related firms collapse as existing bookings had to be canceled, money refunded to clients, destinations closed for future bookings, and major international events canceled until further notice.

Even if the company was able to continue and cover these losses, staff numbers were drastically reduced. For example, Ryanair was ready to resume flights later but 3,000 pilots and crew were to lose their jobs. It was inevitable that companies would have to reduce staff numbers to survive. Some were able to take advantage of government funding schemes to keep staff on reduced pay for the short term at least. While some travel agent services could potentially shift to online and telephone operations, we had already seen that customers were keen to see the travel agent face-to-face. Despite the restrictions, some were positive that travel plans could resume in the near future.

Small-scale hospitality businesses were struggling as they often had limited financial resources to fall back on. If they offered accommodation, guests were likely to cancel. If they were still able to offer some form of limited capacity, restaurant and bar facilities had to be closed. Those running bars and pubs had no income as their doors were shut to customers; then vast amounts of stock had to be destroyed as it became out of date for sale or consumption. And, of course, no travel to the major business areas meant no passing trade for takeaways, coffees, and snacks that the small independent cafes relied on.

Figure 6.1 Phoenicia Hotel in Malta

Did the larger tourist facilities fare better than the small ones? Larger hotel chains were able to keep a few key places open while closing others. Premier Inn, for instance, saw revenue fall by 99 percent in seven weeks (May 2020) and retained 27,000 staff on the furlough scheme while not working, with just 39 of their hotels still open. In addition, this was an opportunity to upgrade or refurbish premises if they were forced to close. For example, the 5* Phoenicia Hotel in Valletta, Malta, was able to carry out significant restoration work during this time, as you can see from the upgraded central lounge area in Figure 6.1. Operating at a much reduced capacity, the hotel saw business travelers as their lifeline during restrictions when many of their regular leisure customers were unable to stay with them.

Reopening Larger Attractions and Theme Parks

Large theme parks and major activity centers and venues were closed during this period, losing revenue from visitors while they still had to pay ongoing maintenance costs. There had been attempts to plan for reopening some tourist destinations. At the time, WishTrip issued guidance for this type of venue, with the reality of the impact of COVID-19 still not obvious as everyone tended to be upbeat about there being an end to restrictions. They were particularly focused on national parks and large open-space venues, outlining the best way to use technology to help compliance with state/national authority standards and convince visitors it was safe to return. Their guidance was based on the technological tools they design, but the principles behind suggestions for reopening successfully apply to everyone.

They stress the need for monitoring social distancing and using GPS-based options for tracking visitor progress around the site to avoid overcrowding or bottlenecks where people are slowed down. A good example is the Everland Resort in South Korea, which changed its program of events, canceled parades, and added extra activities around the site (Wish-Trip). As regular hand washing was a major part of protection for individuals, as well as wearing masks, extra wash facilities were installed.

In the United States, theme parks were aiming to reopen by the summer of 2020, optimistic about a phased return though still aware it would not be the same as before. They accepted that crowds would need to be smaller and controlled more, and some of the iconic elements of a visit to a theme park would inevitably be unavailable. The vision of a new "normal" during the pandemic included social distance spacing while waiting in queues, seats on rides blocked off to keep people apart, all visitors and staff required to wear masks, and temperature checks when entering the park (WP). Even more of a disappointment for visitors, the famous characters that children loved to hug would no longer be able to have close contact.

Disney theme parks in Florida were planned to reopen, the famous Star Wars Stormtroopers now warning visitors to keep wearing their mask and to stay a safe distance from others. They were also canceling parades and fireworks displays, so the atmosphere would clearly be a bit more somber.

Other parks, such as Sea World Orlando and Universal Orlando Resort, were changing one of their most significant features, interacting with their animals, and trying to find ways to control numbers of visitors entering and queuing to see the attractions. Attractions such as the National Zoo in Washington were still deciding if, and when, they would reopen (in 2020) and under what conditions.

Museums stayed closed for now, although the Louvre in Paris went for controlling admissions by prebooking time slots, as did some of the art galleries in London, although this caused extra problems as groups of visitors were then bunched together and struggled to see the exhibits clearly. Managing these logistical problems were always going to present problems, particularly for the most popular iconic attractions around the world.

With extra measures introduced at visitor attractions, and inevitable extra costs involved, it was vital that they found ways to continue operating efficiently. This is an ongoing theme across the industry worldwide, especially as the financial environment has been difficult for so long. We also come back to the need to make the best use of social media to spread the word about changes with new user-generated images and content—see later discussion about trends.

Theaters and arts venues also closed, with significant job losses throughout the entertainment world. For this sector, there had been little sign of recovery by the beginning of 2022 although performances are rapidly getting back to some form of normality.

It is not just hospitality businesses that have suffered, but also the wide range of providers who serviced them. Catering and produce suppliers lost major clients. This extended further to those in construction as major planned rebuild/repair/extension jobs were shelved indefinitely.

Given the closures and collapse of businesses we have discussed so far, the pandemic has obviously been bad—if not catastrophic—for travel and tourism worldwide. However, lockdown brought some unexpectedly positive results. As all forms of traffic reduced, so too did emissions and air pollution levels. Reduced air pollution led to fewer deaths and hospital admissions due to asthma and other respiratory diseases. The striking images (Figures 6.2 (a) and (b)) released by NASA illustrate the vastly reduced emissions and pollution in China due to reduction in the use of vehicles, power plants, and industrial facilities, and a million people in quarantine (NASA).

Skies became clearer with limited light pollution, birds returned to urban areas, and wildlife suddenly became braver. News coverage showed wild goats from the hills wandering down into a nearby holiday resort; the wild Kashmiri goats in Figure 6.3 were seen strolling down streets and munching happily on well-tended garden flowers or hedges. People were encouraged to still go outdoors for exercise, although this was interpreted

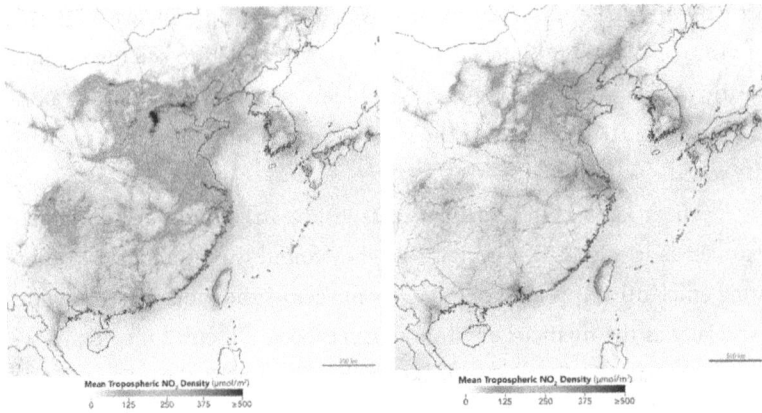

Figure 6.2 NASA images of changes to emissions in China: (a) January 2020, (b) February 2021.

Figure 6.3 Wild Kashmiri goats in seaside resort

differently by individuals. It has led to greater commitment to continuing with cycling, walking, and exercising outdoors when lockdown is over.

When the pandemic started, the world started to recognize the problems of overtourism with damage to the environment, and infrastructure, in the most popular holiday destinations (JJ). Two years of travel restrictions certainly eased the situation, giving tourism businesses time to review how they operate.

The World Travel Market (WTM) Industry Report for 2021, published in 2022, gives many insights into the impact of the pandemic as it is based on major surveys during the latter part of 2021. To summarize the findings:

- At the beginning of 2021, international tourist arrivals into the United Kingdom were down 83 percent in the first quarter of that year.
- The United Nations World Tourism Organization (UNWTO) stated there had been a billion fewer arrivals than the year before.
- ABTA's bookings for the summer of 2021 were down by 83 percent, and around 70 percent of members thought they would have to make staff redundant.
- There were concerns from Airlines UK and the Airport Operator's Association that the United Kingdom was not keeping up with the rest of the world even though they had been so far ahead with the vaccine program. Instead of being the busiest airport in Europe, the London Hub was down to 10th on the scale of busiest.

How It Changed the Way We Travel

CHAPTER 7

What Does the Customer Want?

It was already apparent at the start of the pandemic that tourism was growing, demand was increasing across all age groups, but elements of choice were changing. We also know the pandemic introduced a short, sharp shock to the industry and became a catalyst for action (WTM).

Sustainability

Sustainability has been a feature of discussions about travel and tourism for several years and it is undoubtedly taking on a higher profile as we emerge from the pandemic into an endemic situation. The definition I prefer describes sustainability as:

> fulfilling the needs of the present generation while not compromising future generations' ability to meet their needs. (Trondent)

Whether you are a leisure or business traveler, the choice of transport is a major part of the positive or negative impact on the environment. The airlines are trying very hard to find ways to lessen their carbon footprint, bearing in mind that emissions are greatest during take-off and landing. While a trip might be a bit cheaper if there is a stopover/layover on the way, a nonstop flight is environmentally much better (though likely to also be more expensive). It will be interesting to see whether software currently being developed to assess the carbon footprint for different journeys and types of transport will actually deliver any usable options when the traveler is making their final choice.

We have seen the importance of sustaining local communities that rely on tourism growing, and this has impacted on the changing demand from customers. For instance, nature reserves and national forests in Kenya are trying to involve more visitors to be "immersed" in the experience, not just looking on as an observer. They have already seen signs that travelers want to reconnect with new cultures and nature as they emerge from the confines of the pandemic. At the OL Pejeta Conservancy in Kenya, for example, they have combined farming cattle with the wildlife which means they are able to retain 90 percent of their biodiversity. Their MD, Richard Vigne, told WTM that visitors don't just want to take a ride in a dusty vehicle to see wild animals from a distance, but they want to be engaged with the whole experience of conservation (OL/WTM).

The issue of trying to maintain natural biodiversity in a region has been patchy around the world, but it is becoming more widespread. If it is emerging as an important aspect of a trip potential visitors are looking for, then everyone in the industry will have to ensure they can satisfy the demand in some way. The demand is also growing for evidence that accommodation providers, once they arrive at their holiday destination, are also taking action to be as eco-friendly and sustainable as possible.

Survey Results From 2020 Onwards

Now was the time to take notice of how demand was changing, a time to urgently refocus on what was being offered to the customer. As closures and restrictions took hold, there was, in fact, little choice for customers. By mid-2020, options travelers/tourists were looking for had started to emerge.

At the end of the year, Travelzoo surveyed the 45 to 54 age group, the next generation of mature travelers (STA). This group rated "time to relax/ recharge" higher compared with the general population, but as they are part of the main working-age cohort, they may have felt more stressed by the impact of the pandemic on their work patterns. They were keener than the general U.K. population to take a break abroad than in the home country, and around 10 percent more of this age group said they were more likely to choose a beach holiday or a city break.

The regular Industry Report produced by Silver Travel Advisor gives us a comprehensive view about what the mature traveler is looking for (STA). While the biggest issue for travelers continued to be ensuring they were safe with adequate insurance cover and a successful vaccine program in place, how they define "successful" is not clear. In addition, they said they will continue to be wary until they have seen tour providers operating successfully (again, not defined) for several months before choosing to travel with them.

The later report from February 2021 shows just how eager they were to travel again, based on how they viewed the vaccine program at the time. Saga Holidays was keen to lead on this as they insisted all guests have had both vaccine doses before travel, noting that "98% of our customers said this is what they wanted."

The ITIJ key travel demographic report (ITIJ 2021) found that 38 percent of millennials were likely to lead the way by aiming to travel internationally in 2021, with luxury-end travelers continuing to plan overseas or cruise trips.

Solo travelers had found quarantine to be the biggest barrier for them (Solo Traveler World), with over three-quarters saying they will only travel if no quarantine at the destination and 61 percent only if vaccine is a requirement. There was an even split of 40 percent each for looking to travel in the United Kingdom/Europe or looking for more sustainable travel. The CEO of Overseas Adventure noted that women were the largest demographic for solo travel, describing them as typically "independent and bold."

Travel agents took a hit during 2019–2020, with the Cruise Lines International Association (CLIA) noting that before the pandemic, they were responsible for 75 percent of cruise bookings (CLIA). By 2021, it was clear that they were now a more popular choice from an advice and security point of view. The STA review noted that respondents specifically stated a preference for the smaller, independent travel agency rather than the larger chains.

We had already seen a shift to more eco-friendly travel, in both destination and the means to get there. Interests associated with certain target groups were changing, as was the Bucket List and the way people searched for what was on offer. It is interesting to note how important these changes are for the industry as orders for larger aircraft and the supersized cruise liners dropped or were canceled. This was a crucial time for airlines and statements issued give an idea of how they saw the future for flying.

For example, Sir Ron Eddington, former CEO of British Airways, saw an end to the use of large planes for leisure travel with a fall in demand for connecting flights and a preference for point-to-point flights.

Go Fly said that cut-price airlines have two advantages over the higher priced providers:

1. They can drop prices quickly and spot new potential routes to offer passengers.
2. Their flights are likely to be shorter ones so a positive option for those who would rather take the lesser risk of the virus on a short flight than a long-haul one.

Professor Borenstein from the Hass School of Business at the University of California thought that fares were likely to stay stable for a while, but fare hikes were possible if airlines start to go bankrupt so reducing the number of competitors.

At the same time, Reuters predicted more airlines would convert passenger jets to freight, potentially at a rate of around 36 percent in 2021. However, a report by Martin Armstrong for Statista shows that deliveries of commercial aircraft rose during 2021, showing some recovery for Boeing and Airbus although there is still some way to go.

By the end of 2021, the travel sector was more positive about booking levels starting to get back to what they were at the start of the pandemic. Around half of those in the industry think that numbers will not reach 2019 levels, and around 40 percent believe they will reach or surpass those levels. It will be interesting to see how close they actually are by the end of 2022. It is clear that at least 4 out of 10 businesses in the industry sector (at the end of 2021) think that it will still be a struggle for them during 2022.

There is certainly a pent-up demand for overseas holidays/vacations, 70 percent saying they plan to book at least one break in 2022 and others planning to spend more than they did in 2019. It would seem that the vast majority think they are as well off financially, or even better off, than they were before COVID-19. In addition, there are some still undecided about what to spend any extra money on, so they could potentially be persuaded to travel again.

Marketing Trends and Reaching New Customers

There have been several ongoing studies of social media usage, some of them age-related and some about how the different platforms are used. The pandemic has encouraged greater use of technology to communicate with others, whether between family and friends or between customer and supplier. At the beginning of the pandemic, we were already seeing branding as an important part of marketing for the travel industry (JJ) and this seems to be a continuing theme in the use of social media. As others have said, COVID-19 has been a catalyst for a rethink generally.

The 2021 Social Media Trends report from HubSpot/TalkWalks (HubSpot) is a comprehensive report based on data from a range of sources, so is a useful indicator of how things are changing.

User-generated content (UGC or UGI) had already grown as an element of how travel businesses engaged with existing and potential customers, but with such limited opportunities to travel and explore new destinations, customers were now looking at ways to reformat the material they have.

A clear definition in this report is for "remixing—the art of taking existing formats, templates, or ideas, and recreating them" in a way that reflects their own experiences. Basically, this is the time to increase the options for customers to be involved and explore your "brand" with new types of content. Although not just aimed at the tourism sector, it is suggested that travel and hospitality businesses think about providing their own templates for viewers to add to.

A critical part of this research is the emphasis on the personal touch, information based on real experiences by users rather than something produced formally by the marketing department. This has been around for a while as an integral part of social media platforms that are popular with younger age groups. It does, of course, take away the element of control from the brand's point of view but the templates option gives back a bit of control on the way content is seen.

It is interesting to see that at the time, there was still uncertainty about whether the pandemic would be under some form of control (which we know it isn't) but realization that there will be repercussions for many years.

The 4Cs of COVID-19

The concept of the 4Cs of COVID-19 (cleanliness, contactless, community, compassion) (HubSpot) are mentioned by senior representatives from a range of brands, such as Checkout.com and Digital Academy, and illustrated with the perfect example of KFC dropping their "Finger Lickin' Good" slogan given the implications of the virus! These 4Cs are meant to reflect the concerns of customers when looking at what is on offer. We have already seen the importance of cleanliness and contactless in other surveys of the traveling public.

The most significant trends to take away from this particular research include:

- Aiming to help the customer through the pandemic, to build a connection with them so that the relevant content is based on their concerns.
- The "hard sell" will not work with millennials or younger Generations X and Z as they are looking for more personalization.
- Referring back to the 4Cs, link back to the ones the customer is most concerned about—this may not be the ones you had previously focused on.
- There is frequent mention of nostalgia marketing and possibly rereleasing previous products. We have already seen the popularity of mini cruises and short breaks that feature music from the 1970s to 1990s.
- Some of this popularity for retro and nostalgic elements is also aimed at younger generations where it is new for them, as well as the comfort factor for those who remember it the first time around.

- Return to traditional communication methods that seem to be working now as newsletters are back in favor with consumers—mentioned in other studies too.
- The preference for listening rather than reading has been increasing, hence the rise in popularity of podcasts. For example, 55 percent of Americans now listen to podcasts regularly.

Using Social Media

We often see messages that certain social media platforms are becoming more popular, but evidence suggests that the main ones continue to hold their dominance even when new options arrive. The three biggest platforms of 2021—Facebook, Twitter, and Instagram—continue to be important although there is suggestion that Twitter is losing ground and LinkedIn is gaining.

The current thinking is that Facebook has reached its growth limit, as we can see in Figure 7.1, based on its usage figures for the last quarter year of 2021, with a clear indication that its popularity has plateaued as we go

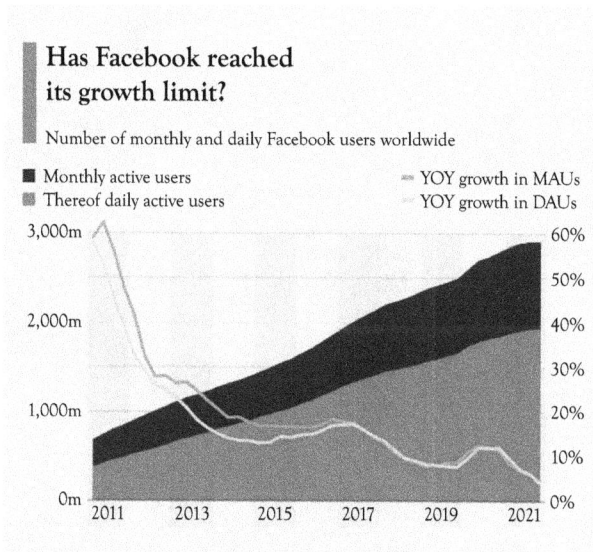

Figure 7.1 Facebook usage chart

Source: Statista

into 2022 (Felix Richter, Statista Infographics Bulletin 5380). The change to Metaverse is seen as a rebranding exercise, possibly because of this. The biggest change for Facebook is active usage by younger age groups and teenagers. Just over a quarter of teenagers now say they actively use their Facebook account, compared with 94 percent of them 10 years ago (Katharina Buchholz Statista 26151)—see Figure 7.2. The crucial point is that all social media platforms need to adapt the features they offer, such as Facebook Horizon or Twitter Voice, to stay relevant.

People are likely to research your brand to see what is on offer and how you are tackling global issues. These are all points that the travel industry is aware of, but it may still be time to reflect on them again.

In August 2021, ATTEST research also highlighted how different age groups were using social media platforms. We know that this element of marketing changes rapidly, but it is useful to see what they see as trends in 2021–2022.

- TikTok had become the favorite platform for Generation Z—those aged 18 to 25—with 56 percent using it every day but note that 47 percent also used Facebook daily.
- Instagram is still popular, with 66.5 percent of Generation Z using it daily.

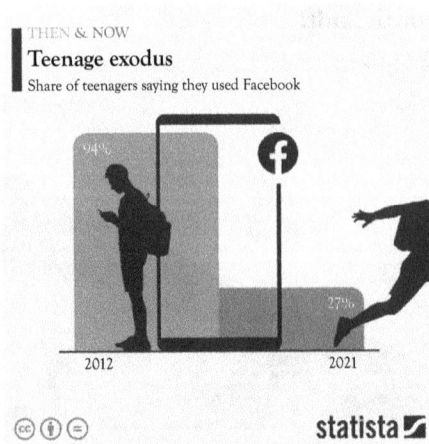

Figure 7.2 Facebook usage by teenagers

Source: Pew Research, Piper Sandler, Business Insider/Statista

- Millennials (age 26 to 40) are not so keen on TikTok, with only 23 percent of them using it every day.
- For Generation X (age 41 to 55), Facebook is still a strong favorite as 68 percent say they use it daily (though note its falling popularity).

ATTEST's later research looked specifically at differences between the U.S. and U.K. consumers when they looked at and recognized brands. As a starting point at the end of 2021, half of the U.K. consumers shopped online for nonfood products compared with 37 percent in the United States. Online shopping is popular across all age groups in Britain, with 46 percent of baby boomers choosing to shop online although U.S. baby boomers prefer to shop in store.

Americans spend more time on social media platforms each day than their British counterparts and are more likely "to interact with brands" when online. A substantial 83 percent of Americans and 75.5 percent of British respondents say they follow and interact with brands on social media.

The Statista Global Consumer Survey in 2021 asked where consumers of all ages from 16 to 64 got "shopping inspiration" from. This gives a useful breakdown of channels that are best to reach customers and inspire them to choose a brand.

Sources of inspiration	% (more than one choice available)
Search engines/ Internet	42%
Friends and family	40%
Social media	37%
Customer reviews	34%

When looking specifically at online use for travel, WishTrip drew some useful findings from the early days of the pandemic. They found that younger age groups, including millennials, expected to see information about destinations online, especially user-generated images (UGIs). They look at social media for inspiration but expect short content as they tend to skim read (Nielsen Norman Group/WishTrip). Wider research, quoted by WishTrip, also suggests that millennials are more connected to their phones than other groups, have travel Apps, and share every aspect of their life online.

They may not be interested in all-inclusive luxury vacations, preferring more off-beat locations to experience rather than just see what the destination has to offer. In other words, they are keen to learn something new on their travels, not dissimilar to what the mature market is looking for. Their phone is used, often daily, to give updates on their trip to family and friends and they spend more on travel-related services than any other group (Phocuswright).

Traveler Behavior

Going forward into 2022 and beyond, postpandemic, we have seen so many changes to what we can, or cannot, do that it has been almost impossible to predict and plan for the long term. Ongoing market research by major players in the travel and marketing industries to identify trends, as well as regular surveys to assess opinions of travelers, does give some indicators to take forward.

The research on Traveler Mix (ADARA), based on three years' data for travel in the United States, produced a new view of what they predicted for 2021 onwards. They identified two major shifts in travel behavior based on hotel categories.

Defining hotel categories as economy, mid-scale, or upscale and luxury, they looked at traveler types based on the highest tier they had previously achieved. These were:

- Novice travelers who were new to booking hotels rather than other types of accommodation;
- Casual travelers who had no real preference or allegiance to any type of hotel;
- Top-tier travelers who took more trips per year (based on hotel bookings) and spent more per year, on average, than the other two types.

In all sections over the three years, they identified that "casual" traveler numbers declined in all hotel categories, with the biggest rise being "novice" travelers across all hotel types. There was less obvious change in top-tier bookings, although numbers overall had declined.

While novice travelers may not be the highest in volume or value, they are on the increase so a category worth recognizing in the future. They appear to be price-sensitive—maybe price-aware is a better description—but not totally if they think they are getting value for their spend.

Not surprisingly, they found the biggest increase in travel demand was for "wide open spaces," including the top-tier groups not always associated with this element of choice, so representing a very real change in demand. Note this research relates to hotel bookings, is not age-specific, and is from 2021, but the findings are a useful benchmark for future trends.

This demand for a return to experiences away from the normal crowded tourist destinations is echoed by USTA who predicted a return to the "Great American Road Trip." People are saying they will feel more comfortable traveling in their own vehicle to places, avoiding the hassle of airports and flights. The humble campervan is again being seen on the open roads, not just in America, so just seeing a scene like Figure 7.3 is likely to bring back memories whatever your age.

They (USTA) see Montana, South Dakota, and North Dakota becoming a favorite choice across all age groups and expect to see a spike in visitor numbers. There has also been a rise in those looking for luxury accommodation with private transport to get them there. This fits

Figure 7.3 The Great American Road Trip

with news from a private jet company, Sentient Jet, who have seen an 80 percent increase in bookings for passengers wishing to travel but avoid the restrictions imposed by regular airlines. They see this as a growing trend in the future.

ABTA reports that bookings for 2022 and 2023 are increasing as stability returns to the sector (Travel 2022 Report). The major trends to look out for are:

- Increased spend on the main holiday/vacation to catch up with missed travel opportunities. While surveys conducted in early 2021 suggested this was not likely to happen, now almost a half of those surveyed are planning to spend more, either through upgrades or by extending their stay.
- As confidence returns, so does the feeling of excitement and adventure. More than a third said they would visit a completely new destination.
- Bucket List destinations are also starting to change but still aim to provide the trip of a lifetime. Among the newer destinations identified are expeditions to the Arctic region and visits to the Galapagos Islands.
- Travel agents will once more become the preferred choice to book a trip, with around 50 percent of travelers saying that guidance they offer will be an important part of their booking decision. This is good news as significant numbers of new customers are already choosing to book their trip through a travel agent.

ABTA also suggests a growing trend will be with those new to the cruising experience. As smaller cruise ships offered new domestic sailings during the pandemic, rather than longer ocean cruises, an increase in demand from new cruise fans has already started. For instance, Fred Olsen started to promote their small ship cruises from September 2021. With the launch of new river and ocean cruise ships in 2022, this is the trend to watch.

Particularly significant is the choice of a package holiday/vacation to add more security and peace of mind. ABTA quotes 78 percent saying that the choice of a regulated package deal was now important or essential.

As we have seen during two years of the pandemic, a crucial element has been the lack of contact with the wider family. Now eager to catch up, the multigeneration holiday is a major trend in 2022 as family groups finally get to meet: Figure 7.4 is a perfect example! This was already a growing segment of travelers before the pandemic became global but was particularly hard hit as meeting with extended family was restricted.

Sustainable travel is high on the agenda for destinations, service providers, and customers. More than 50 percent of customers say this is a big part of how they choose a package from a travel company. For example, a recent YouGov survey found that 30 percent of those in the 25 to 49 age group (including millennials) said they would consider swapping a holiday overseas for one in the home country (the United Kingdom) "to reduce the impact on the environment." ABTA's "Travel for Accommodation" scheme is an interesting development for the future.

Figure 7.4 Multigeneration: meeting up with family

ADARA believes that, based on their research, the widespread vaccine programs will be a significant factor in the number and spread of bookings as they have already seen surges as each new vaccine was announced. Going forward, they believe that the pent-up demand for travel seen in all research areas means tour operators and providers need to make sure they are at the forefront of options once customers start searching. They quote useful examples of travel marketing strategies from flexible booking options to using the work from home/remote work as part of "an amazing vacation!"

The trends in social media usage we discussed earlier are now an essential element of reaching new customers. Keeping track of demand, particularly the way different age groups search for and book a break, will be crucial for everyone in the industry.

While loyalty programs had started to weaken even before the pandemic (JJ), when booking a trip for business, for example, there may still be scope to capitalize on demand for such schemes in the future. The frequent flyer and frequent traveler schemes offered by airlines and hotels seemed to be the most vulnerable to the effects of the restrictions imposed around the world. If you are not able to fly, how can you gain points or air miles? How can you use points accumulated if there are no flights to your chosen destination?

Using a Travel Credit Card gives you points and special status recognition to use later. The Points Guy (WP) agreed that while travel was severely restricted, offering points on this basis does not seem to be much of an incentive for the traveler. He also pointed out that hotels and airlines gained financially from selling miles or points to the credit card companies, so finding some way to overcome the problems was vital.

To keep customer interest in loyalty programs, which have been seen as a positive reward and incentive to book with companies who are part of the scheme, some brands are counting everyday spending on things other than travel to enable special status in the future. Great for the customer as redeemed points on this basis went up by 134 percent for American Express rewards scheme, compared with 2019 figures. Customers were keen to take advantage of this option while it lasted, as it was not likely to continue after the pandemic. A clear sign that this was an attractive option for customers.

In 2021, U.S. restaurant sales were predicted to return to pre-pandemic levels, but the guidance issued in July for guests to wear masks even if fully vaccinated produced a big dip in customer numbers in August.

It was agreed by all major players in the industry that international travel had gone "from bad to worse" compared with 2019 (UN WTO). In 2020, the number of trips was down by 73 percent and in 2021 by 85 percent, with all regions of the world down by between 72 percent and 85 percent; note the Asia Pacific region numbers were down by 95 percent.

Region	Year and percentage drop in number of trips
Global	2020; 73% fewer trips than 2019
Global	2021; 85% fewer trips than 2019
Asia Pacific	2021; 95% fewer trips than 2019

Although U.S. airports had started to get busier, passenger numbers had shrunk from 2.53 million in 2019 to 1.98 million. In addition, the Federal Aviation Administration reported a spike in unruly passengers on flights—an interesting development.

In the United Kingdom, ADARA's research noted that even though staycations had increased during the pandemic, people just wanted to fly abroad again, with Spain and the United States topping the list of preferred destinations. For U.K. travelers, over 40 percent of bookings were for a trip during the next 30 days, and the top five destinations were:

Destination	Stated preference as %
Spain	14%
United States (despite them not allowing British visitors at the time!)	13%
Greece	5%
Portugal	5%
Italy	4%

The cautionary note, as you would expect, is that COVID-19 is still rampant across the globe with new variants appearing and restrictions likely to be applied or relaxed regularly in the foreseeable future. At the same time, some of the most crucial elements of the desire to travel and explore unfamiliar places are the ones we cannot currently enjoy. While we may be able to travel without masks and will go back to having to sit close to others on the journey, will we be too scared to go back to the random hugging, kissing, and general close contact in new surroundings that make a trip special?

How important and, indeed, effective has the vaccine program been for getting us all traveling again? It has been patchy across the globe to be fair, sometimes due to decisions by the government of the day and sometimes down to logistics. The aim was for 60 percent of the world's population to be vaccinated by 2023, with most regions aiming to do so by late 2021 or mid-2022. To meet any goal across every part of the world, you would have to have considerable faith in the basic premise behind it. In this case, it may indeed be extremely optimistic and, I believe, unachievable. The latest figures at the beginning of 2022 confirm this view—see Figure 7.5.

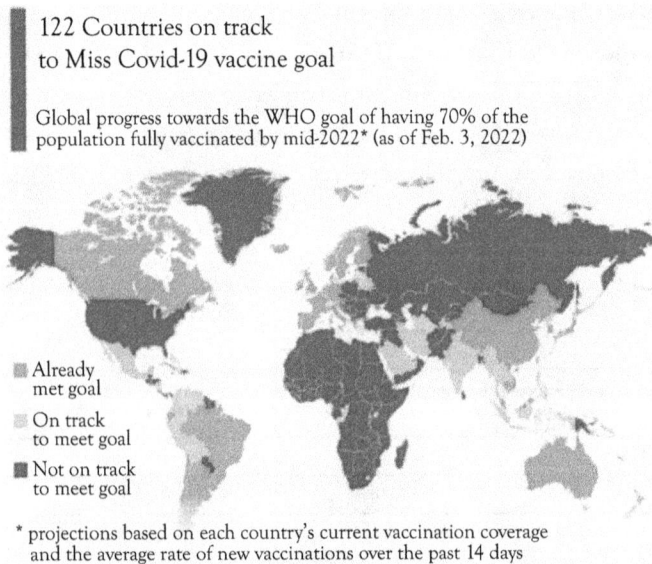

122 Countries on track
to Miss Covid-19 vaccine goal

Global progress towards the WHO goal of having 70% of the population fully vaccinated by mid-2022* (as of Feb. 3, 2022)

Already met goal

On track to meet goal

Not on track to meet goal

* projections based on each country's current vaccination coverage and the average rate of new vaccinations over the past 14 days

Figure 7.5 *Countries on track to miss vaccination targets worldwide*

Source: Our World in Data/Statista

At various times, lists of cities deemed to be safe to visit have appeared with a percentage score. For example, see Table 7.1.

Table 7.1 Cities scored for perceived levels of safety

City	% Score for level of safety
Toronto	82%
Copenhagen	82%
Singapore	80%
Sydney	80%
Tokyo	80%
Amsterdam	79%
Wellington	79%
Hong Kong	78%
Melbourne	78%
Stockholm	78%

The variation between scores for this list of cities is hardly a useful measure, and as we know, outbreaks of the virus are constantly appearing even in those places that consider themselves to be "safe." At the end of August 2021, a map of Europe's safe list of countries to visit and to travel from did not include the United Kingdom as incoming travelers, despite a substantial coverage of the population for both vaccine doses. This has changed by 2022 but there is still no guarantee that things will stay consistent as we start to find the "new normal" and ways to deal with an endemic rather than pandemic situation.

CHAPTER 8

What Are the Biggest Changes Since 2019?

We started this discussion with the question of how a global pandemic changed the way we travel. In reality, the question is much broader than that so we have briefly covered some of these issues. The pandemic has changed the way we live, the way we work and use our leisure time, the way communities operate, and our views of the natural world. All these elements have a direct impact on the way we travel around the globe so none can be viewed in isolation.

So, what have been the biggest changes in our views about travel? There are several elements to consider, including:

- Financial implications
- Attitudes of travelers and personal safety concerns
- Impact on the physical environment
- How booking decisions are made

Financial Implications for Travel

These underpin the majority of decisions about travel, whether at a global, business, or customer level.

Global Implications

We know that for many countries, tourism is a major part of their GDP. They may also have poorer living conditions for the local population, with the majority of people working in travel-related service sectors. From a western point of view, these long-haul destinations have been particularly popular with tourists who then bring in substantial funds. The restrictions associated with the pandemic present difficulties for all governments which impact on travel decisions.

This has been an ongoing discussion throughout the pandemic, particularly in the later part of 2021. At the UNWTO, there is concern that blanket restrictions have not stopped the spread of any of the new variants to date and are actually having a more harmful impact on those who rely on "the lifeline of tourism." With such a negative impact on a country's economic well-being through jobs in tourism and hospitality, it is vital that efforts are made to kick-start recovery and get tourists moving again (UNWTO).

Governments worldwide have had to find ways to support businesses suffering from the impact of lockdowns, staff illness, and travel restrictions, some of them at extreme levels. While it may have seemed short-term at the beginning of 2020, it clearly became apparent that we were all in this for the long term.

As businesses closed, whether temporarily or permanently, there was inevitably lost revenue from income tax, taxes on goods sold, and workers' social insurance contributions. Where workers were laid off or made redundant, for countries where some form of benefit is payable to the unemployed, this extended the demand on central funds.

There has been positive action by some governments offering grants to businesses and new forms of loan to help them over the short term. Where a form of furlough scheme (Coronavirus Job Retention Scheme (CJRS)) has operated, the state contributed up to 80 percent of the normal wage to those who were now unable to work as normal. What was originally seen as another element of a short-term fix soon had to be extended for long periods—in the United Kingdom to September 2021.

At that time, the CJRS ended at 60 percent contribution by the government and 20 percent from the employer, so those still unable to return to work were now on a lower income than before. In the end, 11.7 million jobs were furloughed at a cost of £70 billion to the government.

As expected in the hospitality sectors, pubs/bars and restaurants, accommodation, and food services were the hardest hit, as were younger workers most likely to be employed in these industry sectors.

The U.K. government's own research shows that travel and tourism had the highest use of the scheme with 36 percent of jobs in air transport and 35 percent for travel agencies and tour operators. As this is the sector struggling the most to get back to any form of normal business, we could well see more redundancies now the scheme has ended (UK Parliament Library). The main benefit of the scheme was keeping the number of unemployed down, although there is also a suggestion that up to 10 percent of payments may actually have been fraudulent. Despite this, as the scheme has ended but restrictions are still in place in some form, companies that were struggling at the beginning of the pandemic will seriously need to consider whether staff numbers can be sustained. Unemployment figures will then rise, adding to the financial cost to government.

At the same time in Germany, the existing Short Time Working Allowance, which also allowed staff to work part-time if possible, covered 10 million employees. In France, the Chomage Partiel scheme paid 70 percent of gross salary or 100 percent for those on minimum wage (The Guardian). Ireland had a temporary wage subsidy scheme which started at 70 percent of pay, later rising to 85 percent.

In the United States, the Federal Pandemic Unemployment Compensation (FPUC) scheme paid more than 30 million workers. They included a one-off check payment of $1,200 to all individual single households on less than $75,000 each year, twice that to couples plus an extra allowance per child. In addition, there were calls for the Paycheck Protection Program (PPP) to expand the calculations used for determining loans to now cover all business costs.

Financial Implications for Business

Other financial implications for industry are the delays in large-scale private and government-funded projects that often relate to improved transport links. For individual businesses whatever their size, we have already seen the financial implications as a result of the continuing pandemic, especially for the micro and very small firms.

Imposed lockdowns and closure of nonessential businesses meant reduced footfall so no passing trade and no cash flow—well, only flowing out, not in. General running costs/overheads still had to be paid although there were attempts to freeze costs for premises in some regions. It was especially hard for new start-up firms that had paid out substantial setup costs but now had to close before building any sort of loyal customer base.

If staff were able to work from home instead of a central workplace, that was a positive for the company. But, when this was not the case and staff had to be laid off, the government furlough/short-time payment schemes still left part of the wage bill to be covered by the employer. If staff had to be laid off permanently, there was also a redundancy cost to cover.

In hospitality, lockdown meant stock having to be destroyed as it was now out of date for safe use. It is difficult to quantify the loss of costs of refurbishment and expansion plans as some were able to continue with changes more easily while closed to customers, Premier Inn and the Phoenicia Hotel for instance.

Direct cost implications were highest in travel and tourism, with refunds to customers for canceled trips, potential loss of booking fees with the tour operators, and increased costs to ensure insurance cover against these losses in the future. As we know, some customers were happy to fast-forward their bookings to 2021, 2022, or 2023, others to take a voucher toward future bookings, and some tentative new bookings were made bringing in deposits for future trips.

Finally, an additional cost for industry is increased marketing spend for development of new ways to engage with existing or new customers. Much of this will be related to the changes we have seen in the use of technology for both customer and company.

Financial Implications for the Individual

Any financial impact on the individual inevitably impacts directly on travel and tourism. The furlough schemes were meant to help keep staff on the payroll rather than them losing their job permanently. In most cases, this meant the employer topped up the government payments to the normal wage level. However, this still represented a lower income than before the lockdowns for many workers, which resulted in lower household spend and, in some cases, a build-up of bad debt.

If the employer had to make workers redundant, this leads to lower income after a while. For older workers, the likelihood of returning to work after the pandemic was questionable, given their age, so many chose to take early retirement instead, changing the employment market still further.

Reduced nonessential spend often relates to leisure and hospitality luxuries or delays in making new bookings for vacations/trips. There appear to be positive outcomes for those individuals who found lower household spend during periods of lockdown meant they were better off financially and now had extra funds available to spend on travel when restrictions were lifted.

At an individual level, changes to investments and pension funds can have a major impact on the mature saver, potentially reducing funds available for travel. This can lead to a reduction in the number of trips taken each year, but note their stated views in more recent surveys where this did not appear to be a significant worry for them (STA).

Changing Attitudes of Individuals

Attitudes of individual travelers represent a major change for tourism and hospitality and will continue to have an impact on how travel resumes after the pandemic.

At the beginning of 2020, there was early optimism that this new virus would soon be contained and the pandemic short-lived. People were still positive about traveling in the near future, happy to roll existing bookings forward a year. Attitudes toward the first lockdown restrictions were positive, with the majority happy to follow the rules. In some countries, numbers willing to follow the rules were higher than in others, depending on enforcement procedures.

At a personal level, most people followed the self-isolation rules even though this represented problems for the elderly, those living alone, or those living in poorer areas and conditions. People quickly took to online shopping for both essential and nonessential/luxury goods, leading to an increase in delivery services. There was a rise in the development of local community initiatives to check on vulnerable elderly people living alone, to arrange collection of prescription medicines or essential shopping, and to establish food banks to help those struggling with lower incomes.

For the majority, certainly in the older age groups who were considered to be the most vulnerable to the virus, the vaccination programs were seen as the best way out of the pandemic alongside restrictions on moving around. This group was also more willing to follow the rules than younger age groups, and we did see regular press coverage of conflicts where people refused to follow the safety rules—wearing masks for instance.

But feelings of isolation and the negative impact on an individual's personal well-being became a feature across all ages. Family members unable to mix socially or to visit relatives in medical care establishments, rapidly became a feature of press reports. This has had an impact on the growth in plans for big family reunions once it is possible to travel without restrictions. Remember, all those critical workers in health services were also struggling to cope at a personal level, working long shifts in very difficult circumstances, exhausted staff often unable to get back home to see family (as we can see in Figure 8.1).

Following the "only travel if necessary" requirement, there was increasing anger and frustration at the lack of help from tour operators, and airlines, who refused to honor their own regulations that said they

Figure 8.1 Exhausted hospital surgeon

must refund canceled trips in these circumstances. Clearly, systems were not already in place to deal with cancellations and refunds on this scale, but it did seem that some managed it better than others. This will have a longer-term impact on which operators the customer has more confidence in when choosing to book in the future.

Early on, there was reluctance to book too far ahead, but this timescale has constantly changed throughout the pandemic. As we can see in the section on changes to booking decisions, there has been a significant shift in attitudes, with more emphasis on a staycation in the home country rather than overseas (already starting to be a trend at the beginning of 2020). For those who still want to travel further afield, they are looking for more eco-friendly forms of transport, even if only possible for part of the trip. For example, a flight then train journey once closer to the destination.

Changing Attitudes of Businesses

There have been positive results for businesses with time to rethink how and when employees must travel. More online meetings were effective, so are likely to continue. The scaling-down of large conferences and trade fairs will certainly stay for a long time yet, although implications for the travel industry are not so positive with fewer trips and overnight stays in the conference location.

We have already seen how some companies have had positive feedback about online meetings and events in 2021, and this will certainly be a feature in the future for companies whatever their size. This is not just about producing a webinar and holding virtual meetings via platforms like Zoom, although these have proved to be invaluable for businesses during the pandemic. It will need to be smart, quick delivery in short sections to keep the interest of those viewing online and, as we have had to become more familiar with different online platforms, there will need to be variety to keep the audience engaged.

Compared with larger face-to-face gatherings, the virtual option is seen to be more cost-effective for the business but also has the potential to reach a whole lot more customers. Add the feedback from customers that they often find the whole experience of in-person events tiring and frustrating—trying to fit everything in when the bits you want to see overlap with each other—and you can see the attraction for both sides.

This does not mean the in-person event is dead, as some firms believe it is the most effective way to work with potential clients. For example, the World Travel Market annual event, generally held over three days in London, was presented as a virtual event when required by lockdown restrictions, but in 2021 returned to large-scale face-to-face presentations. For the travel industry, this has been a successful model for tour operators and service providers to meet with representatives from potential destinations and to make connections that will develop in the future.

A business that is keen to get back to in-person events is MOZ with its MozCon conference for marketing professionals. As they say, you cannot really experience the full scope of an event, such as networking, "from your living room" and you are unlikely to get the same feeling of energy and enthusiasm from a virtual event. They also believe smaller networking groups may be the way to get people back into the mindset of actually talking to a person.

The biggest change in the way businesses will approach this question of "what is the best way to get our message across to the widest audience" is through some form of hybrid model. As Bejan from Microsoft suggests (WP), for small or medium-sized businesses, there is likely to be greater value in using the "digital space" as much as possible while accepting there are some who prefer the face-to-face approach. Hence the emerging trend to develop a hybrid conference or event.

From a hospitality/tourism brand perspective, this change can be positive when trying to overcome potential difficulties for attendees at the planning stage, ensuring those who cannot attend for whatever reason are still able to take part. For instance, the Social Media Marketing Conference in 2022 will take place in San Diego supported by a live stream for those following remotely. In this case, the fee to attend virtually is around a third of the price to attend in person for the full three days. For businesses who support events at a specific location, this change will need a rethink about the type of support that might be needed as the visitor numbers will be smaller.

The big conference events may not be aimed at the customer or traveler as the audience, but they are an important way for those from tourism and hospitality to ensure they are meeting changing customer demands.

There are events aimed at the consumer, of course, such as The Travel Show, Food and Drink Show in the Lake District, the Good Food & Wine Show in Australia, and EPCOT International Food and Wine Festival in the United States. It is likely that virtual elements will be increased for these types of shows too, including pre-event competitions, live video broadcasts and podcasts, and onscreen demonstrations to reach the wider audience. It will be useful to look back at these shows after 2022 to see if they were able to include a virtual element, and if so, how successfully.

The Physical Environment

The physical environment has become a critical issue throughout the pandemic as there have been so many changes globally since the pandemic began.

There is greater awareness of the environmental impact of travel and tourism as these ceased due to large-scale lockdowns. As traffic volumes reduced in towns, there seemed to be a rapid rise in wildlife wandering into urban areas which no longer posed a threat of injury. Reduced pollution and improved air quality, as cars and heavy vehicles sat silent at their home base and skies were virtually empty of aircraft, led to clearer skies, birds returning, and reduced lung damage for many residents.

For the travel industry, increasing awareness of the impact of an individual's carbon footprint is significant, whether this is related to the destination or the journey to get there. This will be a factor in the way customers now consider what is on offer, and how a tour operator or travel agent deals with it will influence their final decision. We continue to see growing concern about environmental damage to the most popular Bucket List destinations around the world. Choices of these destinations were starting to change as early as 2020 when the pandemic took hold (JJ) so this is a great opportunity to consider new and exciting destinations that the customer will see as a "must-see" trip of a lifetime.

Changing the Way We Book a Trip

Of all the changes to travel due to the pandemic, the way customers search for and decide which trip to book is a critical issue.

There was optimism early on, then resignation, followed by a reluctance to book anything. The traffic light system introduced to suggest safer destinations was intended to help visitors make a choice but instead it just caused more confusion.

In fact, for those already waiting to get away on holiday/vacation, once a list was published with new "safe" destinations added, spikes in bookings quickly appeared. It is not clear why people were prepared to book a trip to destinations on the Red list, deemed to be unsafe for travelers, despite the likelihood that they were in greater danger of contracting COVID-19 or would have to stay in quarantine for 14 days on their return. It seems that people were desperate to get away at any cost.

There is still an emphasis on personal safety, with potential customers wanting to know that COVID-19 protocols are being followed, including wearing masks during the journey and the need to show proof of vaccination. In countries where progress on their vaccination programs is slower, this may be an issue but it is a growing requirement for overseas travel. Both UNWTO and World Health Organization have urged countries not to "use vaccination status as the sole condition for welcoming tourists back" especially when rates of vaccination are still uneven around the world.

As customers are looking for as much reassurance as possible before they make a final booking decision, there is increased demand for the services of a travel agent rather than going ahead with booking direct with a tour company online. Note there is evidence that the tour provider's online presence is still a critical factor in the final choice of package, as is the need for protection of the booking such as that provided by ATOL.

Customers are already thinking about choosing packages with a lower environmental impact on the destination or from the means of travel. Tour operators and hospitality venues have been using this time to rethink what they can offer and where there is a real contribution to local communities, especially where relaxation, well-being activities, and spa facilities are the theme, such as Pulo Cinta Eco Resort (Figure 8.2). Looking for tour operators or agents committed to these elements, and helping the local population, is also a growing trend.

Forward bookings to late 2022 and into 2023 increased, particularly for the planned big trips. There are constant changes in timescales for prebooking, depending on the perceived spread of the virus and infection rates. In the middle of 2021, last minute booking around two weeks

Figure 8.2 Pulo Cinta Eco Resort Photo

before travel was more popular than three months in advance. As you might expect for this summer period, this coincided with changes to the safe list and school holidays so family groups were more likely to book than the solo traveler (ADARA).

As the last two years have seen such a sizeable increase in the use of online sources for researching and buying products or services, across all age groups, this also applies to booking trips. There is concern that while customers are confident when booking vacations/trips online, they are less happy that there are fewer staff at airports, stations, and destinations, to provide face-to-face care and support. Despite some optimism about the rapid increase in bookings, the airlines were not, in fact, able to accommodate the rise in passenger numbers resulting in cancellations and chaos at airports in the summer of 2022. There is no doubt that this will be an essential element of choosing a tour operator in the future.

Tour operators have worked hard to develop exciting new destinations that represent an adventure and a big trip of a lifetime experience. Often in more remote areas, such as the Arctic regions or high mountain ranges, they do need to consider the concerns of travelers about the environmental impact. Again, a difficult balance between what is available and what the traveler wants.

Figure 8.3 Venice now has restricted access for visitors

CHAPTER 9

Where to Next for the Travel Industry?

By May 2020, everyone was looking for easing of travel restrictions to be "timely and responsible" so that the economic and social benefits we expect from tourism can be seen again. However, such a return must also be sustainable. As we know, this was not to be at that time as we continued to see falls and spikes in infection and death rates as new COVID-19 variants appeared, and restrictions on the movement of people became tighter or relaxed depending on which country you were in.

Travel Trends

The ADARA Travel Data Infographic for 2022 considers U.S. travel trends highlighting the top 10 destinations booked in 2021 as those in Table 9.1.

Table 9.1 Top 10 destinations for trips within the United States

Position	Destination
1	Orlando
2	Los Angeles
3	Miami
4	New York
5	Phoenix
6	Tampa
7	Dallas Fort Worth
8	Honolulu
9	Denver
10	San Francisco

Note that these are domestic trips within the United States.

Over half the trips booked were for just one or two days, with 36 percent booking a break between three and six days, all domestic rather than overseas.

For overseas vacations, the top ten destinations for U.S. travelers are an interesting mix: just two European countries included, as you can see from Figure 9.1.

Comparing hotel booking categories for 2019 to 2021, luxury hotels went up a little in 2020 by 10 percent, then reduced slightly to 6 percent, so no notable change. Using their definition of upscale class hotel accommodation, the rates stayed the same for 2020 and 2021 at 67 percent of total bookings, economy class hotels stayed around the same as before, but mid-scale hotels stood at a higher rate of 23 percent of the total.

The World Travel Market report considers emerging destinations for 2022, including Saudi Arabia. It found that 40 percent of U.K. adults said they would consider Saudi Arabia for a holiday, with more than half the businesses questioned planning to have "some" dealings with them, ahead of Italy or Greece. Although the country had started to issue tourist

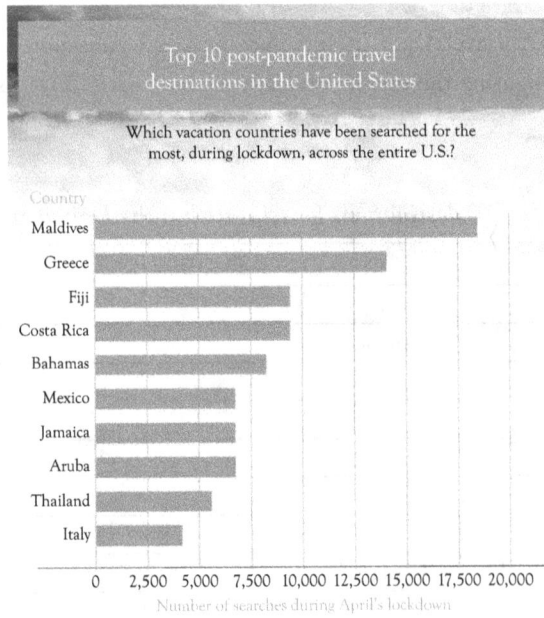

Figure 9.1 Top 10 postpandemic overseas destinations

Source: Insuremytrip.

Figure 9.2 Mosque in Saudi Arabia

visas at the end of 2019, suspension of visits due to COVID-19 means that the first tourists were not back in Saudi Arabia until August 2021.

Not just expanding visitor attractions, such as the stunning mosque in Figure 9.2, they have invested substantially in global sports events that we know are an important part of attracting large numbers of overseas travelers. For example, Japan hosting the Rugby World Cup was a successful travel experience that brought in thousands of new visitors in 2019 (JJ). Both cruise liners and escorted tour providers, such as Explore, are considering including Saudi Arabia in future itineraries.

America, Canada, Europe, Mediterranean countries, Australia, and southern Asia remain as popular destinations, although note that tourists had already started to look for new experiences as the pandemic began. Surveys show that for U.K. travelers, Europe is the top destination with Spain as the favorite choice once again. Still popular with British tourists are France, Greece, and Italy. Brand USA says that there is also a strong base of potential travelers who are keen to visit United States to see family or just to experience the sights.

Favorite types of vacation emerging now are the traditional beach or poolside spots to just sit and relax after what we know have been a stressful few years, with city breaks following closely behind in the list of choices. Comments from the most recent survey reports suggest that around three-quarters of respondents, across all age groups, agreed that we should continue to wear masks onboard a plane, and at the start of 2022, the majority of the major airlines continued to impose the rule.

Other trends include choosing shorter journeys over long-haul flights or ocean cruising, preferring smaller planes and cruise ships from a virus-protection point of view. For instance, American Cruise Lines has made the move to smaller catamaran-style vessels (Travel Weekly January 22). While fans of cruising largely remain keen, river cruising on smaller ships is a growing preference.

WTM also identified COVID-19 as the "catalyst for responsible tourism" and there is already evidence that the travel industry is taking this seriously, not least in order to supply growing demand from customers (JJ). For instance, we had seen earlier predictions of the growth in staycations globally and, despite the slowdown during the pandemic restrictions, they continue to be a popular option.

We have seen trends identified for what the customer is likely to be looking for, and once it is deemed to be safer to travel again, the multigeneration options will need to grow further. The options may be more focused on the staycation, but as so many families are spread around the globe, the need to get together will, perhaps, be more about the type of accommodation than the destination. It has been suggested that the big resorts losing out on conference and event bookings should market their facilities for big family reunions (Hello! 2021), especially if they are close to the sea. The big family reunion that includes a beach, as in Figure 9.3, is certainly near the top of the list of options.

There were interesting comments from Advantage Travel Partnership, representing 750 U.K. travel agents, around the middle of 2021 when future travel was still uncertain. While the shift to staying closer to home was good news for more rural, less popular tourist destinations,

Figure 9.3 Big family reunion on the beach

this shift to staycation threw the spotlight on the negative implications for local residents.

In September 2021, it was clear that demand for these popular destinations far outstripped supply and it was unsustainable going forward, both from an infrastructure perspective and that of the tourists. If, as we had already seen in survey reports, the customer was looking for more sustainable holiday/vacation trips, this should surely also apply to the home country.

While this trend could lead to an extended holiday season, rather than the traditional peak in July and August, this involves wider rethinking on the way destinations are promoted and what they can offer over the long term. During the summer of 2021, there were calls for people to book 2022 and 2023 vacations as soon as possible, with so many popular destinations already fully booked. The Silver Travel report had already identified new booking trends for longer holidays, increased off-peak booking, big trips with multigeneration family groups, and booking further ahead than in previous years.

Travel industry leaders noted their own view of trends going forward, depending on their sector (STA). There are clear patterns emerging for 2022 onwards, including the following highlights from each sector.

Ocean cruising: There has always been a base of loyal cruise guests who are keen to get back on board and 25 percent of the mature travelers expected to sail again by the end of 2021. Companies such as Celebrity Cruises expect to see more multigeneration bookings in the future as families finally get together again. The shift during 2021 to shorter cruises around the coast of the home country, rather than longer ocean cruising, has been seen as a positive outcome for the industry, also introducing new customers to the experience. It has been an opportunity for long-standing cruise companies to adapt what they offer—for instance, the smaller cruise ships introduced by Fred Olsen based on concerns expressed by potential customers during the pandemic.

The specialist cruise market, such as Noble Caledonia, has continued to focus on the mature market who they see as enquiring and, therefore, interested in a specific topic or purpose for their cruise rather than just a general one. They are already taking bookings for special interest cruises in 2022–2023. River cruising has remained a popular choice, again as a smaller ship with fewer passengers, so it will be interesting to see how soon it can get to previous booking levels. The chart by Cruise Market Watch (Figure 9.4) gives a clear picture of how passenger numbers collapsed but started to recover in 2021.

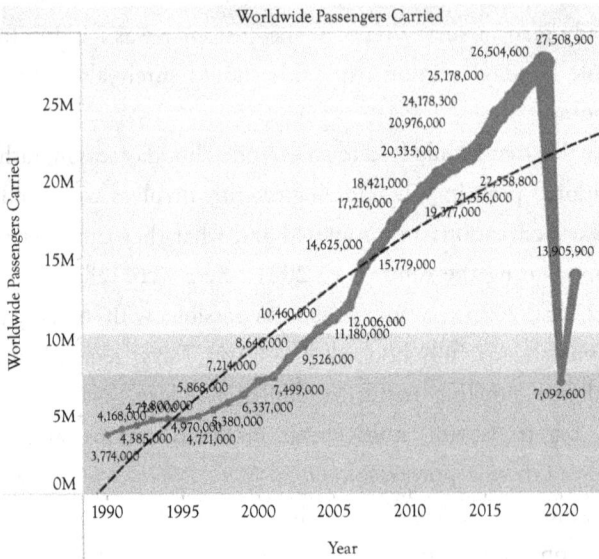

Figure 9.4 Cruise passenger numbers till 2021

Trains: The rail holiday market is growing, with demand for "independent, customized, flexible holidays" by rail often linked to luxury train journeys as a special treat—back to the notion of "Revenge Travel." Railbookers, for example, also found that 85 percent of customers who booked with them during the previous year were new clients so a positive sign for the future (STA). Longer train journeys, usually at the luxury end of the market, are also seen as a positive way to reduce the carbon footprint while continuing to see and experience local cultures.

Coach travel is starting to recover from the restrictions, with the majority of customers booking a trip in the home country rather than overseas, although this is likely to change as travel restrictions are eased. In the escorted tours market, there was growing optimism that touring in Europe would be back on track by the middle of 2021, although this has not been the case. Escorted tour operators such as Cosmos Tours have seen more demand for smaller groups, rural tours, and the fully organized coach tour option for 2022.

City breaks continue to be popular, with the latest trends seeing clients choosing to upgrade and/or extend their stay, again choosing to go with smaller groups. We have seen how the staycation has expanded rapidly, particularly with multigeneration groups, so this pattern will continue, at least in the short term. This growth in bookings for the villa rental market is set to continue (see comments about Airbnb trends) with larger family groups, and those who want to combine remote working with a vacation, looking for long duration stays. The added bonus to such long stays is that the financial contribution to the local economy, through tourism, will increase.

The Bucket List

The Bucket List is a constant reference point in relation to travel so it is interesting to see the trends emerging. Previous Bucket List favorite destinations, such as South America, Africa, Australia, and Canada, are likely to take longer to get back to previous numbers and demand to recover. Note that Venice, a popular Bucket List destination, may not be so accessible in the future as it has banned large cruise ships and is considering charging tourists from summer 2022. There were already signs of its concerns about the structural impact of overtourism before the pandemic, so these moves are not unexpected.

Typical Bucket Lists, such as those on the signpost in Figure 9.5, are regularly featured in leisure- and travel-related publications and online. For example, *Hello! Magazine* in 2021 published their list of 17 landmarks you must see, though not in any particular order, including some more unusual choices such as Alcatraz. Some interesting suggestions can be seen in Table 9.2.

As these are the special trips, the long-awaited adventures to see what the world has to offer, the problems due to pandemic restrictions may have just delayed trips, so booking well ahead to 2022 and 2023 is the most likely option for many. But also remember that the long-haul journey has seen reluctance on the part of potential customers so we will have to see how far demand builds again by the end of 2022.

Meeting Customer Demands

Pricing and affordability will always be a potential problem, and around 70 percent of U.K. consumers surveyed thought that this was a concern for the future. Decreasing fees for flights and hotels that were introduced

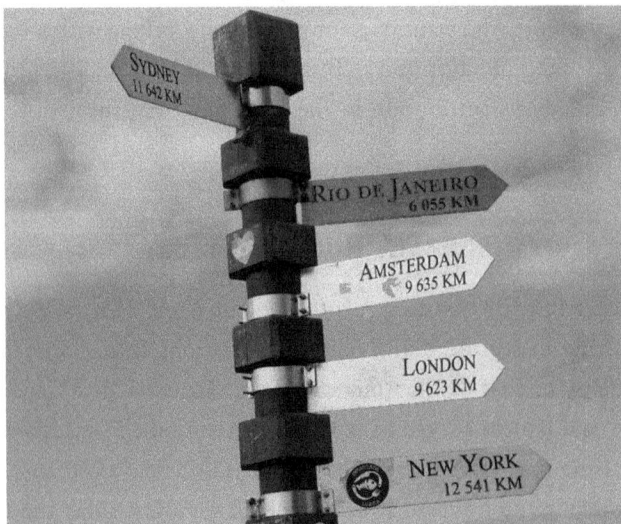

Figure 9.5 The Bucket List signpost—where to next?

Table 9.2 The Bucket List—17 landmarks you must see

Landmark	Country
The Eiffel Tower	Paris, France
Angkor Wat temple	Cambodia
Sydney Harbor and Opera House	Australia
The Great Wall	China
Machu Picchu	Peru
The Colosseum	Rome, Italy
Taj Mahal	Agra, India
Sheikh Zayed Grand Mosque	Abu Dhabi
Empire State Building	New York
Basilica of the Sagrada Familia	Barcelona, Spain
Alcatraz	San Francisco
Vatican City	Italy
Christ the Redeemer statue	Rio de Janeiro
Duomo Cathedral	Milan, Italy
Plaza de Espana	Seville, Spain
Golden Gate	San Francisco
Parliament Building (I would add the Opera House as well)	Budapest, Hungary

during the pandemic cannot, realistically, continue. At the beginning of 2020, travel experiences were viewed positively by most travelers across all age groups. Apart from the long waiting times at some airports, the journey was an enjoyable part of the whole trip. Customer service was at a high level and customers felt like they were being taken care of by staff.

At the time of writing in 2022, as flights have resumed to many destinations worldwide, there have already been scathing reviews about the whole travel experience (LinkedIn). One of the biggest complaints has been about low staff numbers, followed by poor care for the customer at various stages of the journey.

It would be a pity if the excellent levels of care and customer service we enjoyed, and expected, prepandemic are lost due to poor systems and low staffing levels as we go forward through 2022 and beyond. While technological systems may have performed well during the restrictions experienced since 2019, from the industry point of view of course, for the customer there is still a wish for the welcoming, personal touch at different points in the journey.

Self-service kiosks are fine, but as we have all seen, there still needs to be a person there to sort out problems at times. Often the time this takes with one customer could have been used more productively by one staff member just serving several customers quickly and efficiently. Pretravel is the ideal area for automated systems as more people now order online as a normal part of their shopping habit, due to the pandemic—see the chapter on what has changed.

There have been changes at airports since the beginning of 2020, many relating to the way passengers move through the space. Some were expected, such as one-way systems and controlling how people queue, with more reliance on online check-in facilities. Retail outlets were closed and comfortable waiting areas for passengers were blocked off or completely removed. Sanitizing stations became the norm and were generally welcomed by those who were willing to venture out to travel. There was also general acceptance that contactless was the way to go for everything.

What of the "new normal" as we come out of the pandemic and resume some form of travel similar to how it was at the end of 2019? Customer demand has to be acknowledged as we shift from the most extreme restrictions imposed, and yes, it does mean that the travel industry must balance this desire for things to be like they were with their own business needs.

As part of its regular research updates, ADARA's Rebounding report provides fascinating insights to booking choices for travel. It has seen that booking patterns have fluctuated depending on patterns in the virus statistics and subsequent decisions by governments about restricting travel. It is, however, hopeful of a positive rebound for tourism going forward in 2022.

For instance, early in the pandemic, the last-minute booking of 15 days or less prior to travel was fairly consistent but spiked to over 40 percent of total bookings as everyone became concerned about booking too far ahead. By the end of 2021, bookings at more than 90 days in advance had seen a significant upturn.

With a large land mass to accommodate domestic travel, North America did see signs of recovery with an upturn in hotel bookings, although this changed as lockdowns (particularly March and November 2020) were imposed. Given the changes in their choice of destination noted earlier, and the growing appreciation of the home country by many nations that suddenly found they couldn't travel abroad, it is likely that demand for staycation will continue to grow.

For trip duration, the ADARA research identified clear changes in how long customers were planning to be away from home. There are some interesting comments from ADARA on interpretation of these figures, as they may reflect those having to work from home choosing to "work from anywhere," rather than fitting a holiday/vacation into a set time slot then returning to the workplace. There were also examples where people needed to leave their usual accommodation to visit outside their own region, often to care for family members who were struggling to cope at this tough time.

CHAPTER 10

The True Impact of a Global Pandemic on Travel and Tourism

At the beginning of 2020, a major coronavirus flu epidemic emerged and made travel to and from China and East Asia almost impossible. As the virus spread globally, at an unprecedented rapid pace, there was a significant, and in many cases devastating, impact on all travel plans, whether for leisure or business, and for tourist destinations all around the world.

People were convinced that it was likely to be a short-term inconvenience and there would soon be a return to 2019 options for travel. No one could foresee how far reaching the pandemic would be or what the long-term impact could be. We have seen that once the first wave of infections and deaths was over, people were optimistic that a new version of normal would be in place by the end of 2020. In particular, plans were being made to travel again in 2021 in pretty much the same way as before the global pandemic took hold.

There had been over 200 million people affected by COVID-19 by August 2021. Between January 2020 and September 2021, we saw sobering statistics concerning the impact of the COVID-19 virus. The speed of infection was rising, taking 10 weeks to go from 30 million to 60 million but only 6 weeks to go from 120 million to 150 million. By the end of 2021, after two years of ups and downs, peaks in numbers of infections or deaths, it was clear that any optimistic thoughts about an end to the pandemic were not realized.

At the same time, just under 50 percent of people surveyed believed that someone close to them would be infected (Wales Government). More people said that it was no longer a case of knowing someone somewhere who may have been infected, but it was definitely getting "closer to home" as new strains such as Omicron took hold and rates of infection rose. Although the new Omicron variant spread rapidly with, apparently, higher infection rates, it did not necessarily result in more severe consequences for those who were infected. The chart in Figure 10.1 gives a striking picture of how extreme this surge was.

Globally there were still differences in rates of infection, hospitalization, and death but it was not always clear why there were such differences.

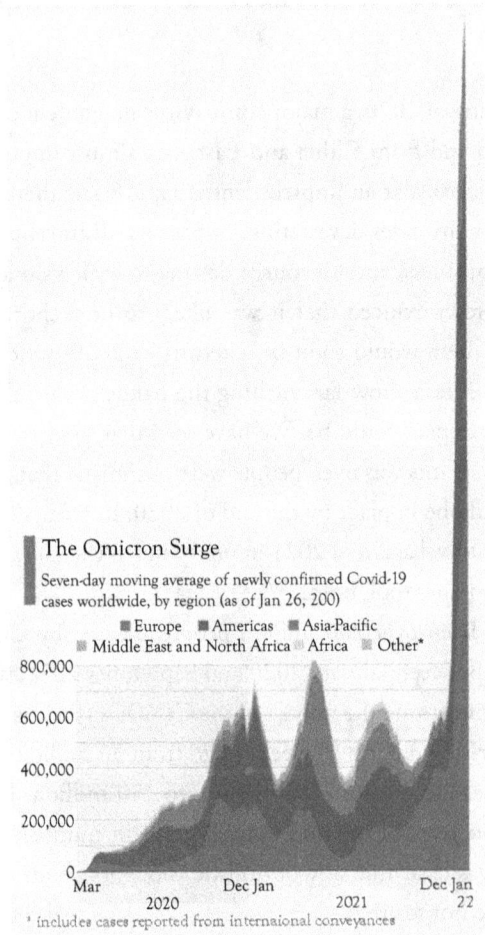

The Omicron Surge

Seven-day moving average of newly confirmed Covid-19 cases worldwide, by region (as of Jan 26, 200)

■ Europe ■ Americas ■ Asia-Pacific
▨ Middle East and North Africa Africa ▨ Other*

includes cases reported from internaional conveyances

Figure 10.1 Surge in Omicron cases in 2022

includes cases reported from international conveyances
Source: World Health Organization/Statista.

By September 2021, the United States had the highest numbers with 42 million cases recorded and 670,000 deaths. The world's second highest death toll was in Brazil with 590,000 and Mexico came in fourth at 270,000. These positions change very quickly so it is just a snapshot as Russia and France also saw large numbers of people affected. The most recent statistics can be found on BBC News online Covid map (BBC news/world online).

On the other hand, by the end of 2021, South Africa showed significant reductions in all case numbers though less extreme protective measures seem to have been introduced by the government. Germany had major restrictions and protection measures in place though numbers did not reduce very quickly.

Australia and New Zealand were still operating lockdowns though other countries had eased the restrictions, while in Europe it is believed that the high level of vaccination among the population helped to keep spikes in cases and deaths lower.

As we have seen in earlier discussions, ongoing research with travelers across all age groups during 2020 and 2021 showed that the initial enthusiasm to get back out there and see the world had waned. The picture was now looking bleak.

So, even at the end of 2021, confusion still reigned among the public and governments worldwide. In turn, travel and hospitality sectors were, again, at the forefront of restrictive measures with devastating consequences for an industry already struggling to survive.

In contrast to actions by other governments, the U.K. government removed the majority of the most restrictive protection measures over the 2021 Christmas and New Year period, resulting in the highest levels of infection rates since the first and second waves of the pandemic.

There seemed to be no clear political lead on the best way to deal with the spread apart from reliance on the vaccine and booster programs and the assumption that the "public" could be relied on to act in a sensible way. Clearly not the case as thousands traveled from their own region, where bars and clubs were closed, across to England where they could celebrate with no restrictions! All restrictions were lifted in the United Kingdom in March 2022.

In February 2022, coronavirus statistics were quoted as follows (Statista):

- The United States had seen 78 million cases with 926,029 deaths.
- India had over 42 million cases and 502,905 deaths.
- Brazil had recorded the highest number of cases in Latin America with over 26 million cases and 632,289 deaths.
- France had recorded almost 21 million cases and 132,506 deaths.
- The United Kingdom had nearly 18 million cases and 158,318 deaths, the highest number of deaths in western Europe.
- Italy had over 11 million cases and 148,771 deaths.

Also see Figures 2.2 to 2.4 in Chapter 2.

During 2020, the author was looking closely at strategies for targeting the mature travel sector (JJ). Before the pandemic took hold, hospitality and tourism were the industries showing real growth in a buoyant market. By the time the book was completed at the beginning of 2021, tourism was hardest hit by travel restrictions imposed across the world. As we move out of the pandemic stage into one where we have to live with COVID-19, it is time to agree what the new "normal" will be.

CHAPTER 11

Living With a
New "Normal"

The global pandemic that spread rapidly around the world at the end of 2019 has had a major impact on everyone's life. Originally viewed as a short-term inconvenience, it soon became a long-term disaster. Now well into 2022, new variants of the virus still appear, with numbers of infections and death rates fluctuating worldwide though much lower than during the height of the pandemic. After more than two years of developments in the way COVID-19 has changed our views of travel, it remains to be seen what the accepted "new normal" will be.

Early optimism soon gave way to resignation and recognition that travel options were seriously reduced around the world. Initially, there was reluctance on the part of tour operators to accommodate changed plans and cancellations. This was also the case with some airlines who made it difficult for passengers to change their flights, whether this was due to a companion's illness or them feeling unwell themselves. However, it was clear that in order to survive in the future, this would need to be a crucial part of any marketing strategy for firms that wanted to retain a customer base.

One of the biggest problems for travelers everywhere, but particularly in the United Kingdom, had been the "traffic light system" where places deemed to be safe to travel to changed overnight. Trips had to be canceled at the last minute and people were stranded all around the world, unable to get home before the new 14-day quarantine period kicked in. The quarantine requirements were unacceptably expensive, often costing more than the holiday had done.

Just changing destinations on the lists, and the travel requirements, was enough to get people back on track and ready to book a well-earned break. Add the widespread vaccination program and there seems to be no reason why travel cannot get back to its prepandemic levels.

Expectations of leisure customers changed during 2020–2021, moving from disappointment and frustration to a pent-up demand to travel again by the beginning of 2022. Customers were prepared to transfer existing bookings to a year ahead, or even two, but they were now looking for health and safety protocols to be in place both on the journey and at the destination.

While tourism, travel, and hospitality industries have been the hardest hit, with smaller-scale operators seeming to endure the bulk of closures and redundancies, tour operators and major industry players have been forced to rethink what they offer and how they communicate with potential customers.

All providers have been forced to revisit their original focus and client expectations by tailoring what they offer to meet the critical elements of:

- Long-haul travel versus shorter distances;
- The individual's carbon footprint and environmental impact on places they visit;
- A feeling of losing out on time available to fulfil the personal Bucket List.

Around the world, countries introducing "no travel" policies for internal travel, as well as cross-border journeys, made it difficult for the local population as well as visitors. Countries were added to, or removed from, Safe Travel lists at short notice adding to the confusion. Can we travel to Europe to see family? If we get there, will we be able to get home? What COVID tests are needed before/during/after travel?

Fast forward to 2022, with new variants of the virus plus reintroduction of sometimes extreme travel restrictions, we can see how everyone globally questions political and medical expertise that rapidly became more confusing. Despite the earlier requirement for those traveling from and to the United Kingdom to pay for expensive PCR testing at several stages of the trip, it became clear that this had negligible impact on the spread of the later 2 variant Omicron.

Finally, in January 2022, the need for PCR testing when entering the United Kingdom was removed leaving a lateral flow test by day two of arrival as the requirement. Note this also had to be a paid version of the test, rather than the existing free one provided by the

National Health Service (NHS), although no one has any idea why this was the case.

These changes were welcomed by the International Air Transport Association as "long overdue" and the World Travel and Tourism Council also thought it would be a positive boost for the industry. With wider costs of living rising, as well as uncertainty about disruption to travel plans (Travel Weekly report 2022), there is growing concern that flying is becoming too expensive and ultimately just for the wealthy, a sentiment we had already heard from others.

For the travel industry, the removal of testing requirements quickly had a positive effect on travel plans. The flight booking site Skyscanner said 2022 was likely to be a bargain year for travel as they had found examples of prices around 70 percent cheaper than in 2019. At the luxury end of the market, Kuoni was predicting bookings would be close to 90 percent of the 2019 levels. Removing these restrictions has reduced unnecessary additional costs for holidaymakers, so has been broadly welcomed. We will have to wait and see how effective it is as a boost for the sector by the end of 2022.

As early as May 2020, survey respondents were starting to doubt how soon things would get back to any sort of normal, with around a third thinking it might be better to travel in 2021 but a further third believed it would be at least 2022 before they would be confident to travel widely. However, while feedback from major tour operators and service providers suggested more positive views about future travel than in the previous three months, travel chaos during the summer of 2022 shows this optimism to be misplaced.

Whatever industry sector you are in, the new version of normal is still stubbornly difficult to identify. For travel and tourism, where forward projections are vital, this is particularly difficult.

Will we still want to travel and explore the world once the new normal becomes the norm? The signs are that *yes*, of course we will. It remains to be seen what the sector will look like at the end of the crisis for both business and leisure travelers. As we have seen with the shift to connecting with customers via online platforms, as well as face-to-face through a rise in demand for dealing directly with a travel agent, the leisure sector will be easier to track and measure activity as we move forward.

For the business sector, there are two distinct areas to consider. One is the recovery plans for tour operators, those who run hospitality establishments, the travel providers, and everyone who supports them. The critical thing now is convincing potential customers that it is safe to travel—the priority listing in all the research studies—and ongoing cleaning protocols are in place in venues they visit. Hotels and accommodation providers are already working hard to get systems in place that are enough without appearing to be too clinical. We come back to how the customer sees the whole experience of travel and what they want to feel when taking the journey—the excitement and anticipation we used to feel rather than the stress and disappointment of the last two years.

For the business traveler, it is not so clear. As organizations have seen they can still operate with employees/workers based away from the central company location, still meeting project targets, and with lower travel costs as no one moves around the country or overseas, there will continue to be an emphasis on the potential for more homeworking. There are already signs that some are happy with this arrangement—that they are content to work at a distance, and would like to continue on this basis for at least part of their work time each week.

In other areas, there have been trial runs for workers to move to a four-day week at a central workplace, with no pay reduction, instead of their normal five days, to see whether this leads to increased productivity. Based on the results of how workers were able to meet targets set when homeworking, this looks like it may indeed be a success for some sectors. Feedback from these trials includes the point that they have an additional day away from the workplace and, therefore, more leisure time.

Linking this with providers of services that rely on workers visiting hotels, the local footfall as they pass local small cafes or delis on their way to work, and local transport links such as taxi services, there are still some concerns about whether the situation with business travelers can ever return to prepandemic levels.

When we include the move to holding virtual or hybrid versions of larger conferences rather than face-to-face, the evidence suggests this will become part of the new normal without dealing with lost trade for all the travel-related companies who enable such events to happen.

For business-to-business organizations in these sectors, the hybrid approach to meetings will inevitably continue into 2022 and beyond. There will still be examples of all forms of events, depending on the type of business. For travel sectors, this is likely to be a combination for business customers through hospitality-related shows and exhibitions. We know that the critical issue is what the customer wants and expects from this line of communication.

Fresh marketing initiatives will be needed to accommodate such fundamental changes to attitudes, buying habits, and choices consumers make as their own circumstances change. Demand will grow, potentially in significant peaks in numbers, although it is unlikely it will return to pre-2020 levels for all sectors.

The Bucket List could actually be the most significant indicator of what the customer will expect and demand from the travel industry in the future. It will also be an indicator of how important the sector is in safeguarding the global natural environment.

Finally, there is the question of how Brexit has impacted travel and tourism sectors. With both Brexit and a global pandemic to deal with, it is not easy to say which has had the greater or lesser impact. There have been significant changes related to passports and immigration, insurance cover at home and overseas, and all forms of cross-border travel requirements, due to the withdrawal from the European Union. Breaking down the information to decide which has had the biggest negative impact will be an ongoing discussion for some time yet.

However, the latest report by World Travel Market (WTM 2021) highlights several trends for 2022 and beyond. Crucially, their predictions for preferred destinations, types of vacation and means of travel, and the wish for more sustainable travel, all directly reflect the trends identified for the mature traveler at the end of 2020.

It appears that for the mature market at least (defined as 50+ with further segmentation to 60+ and 70+), restrictions during the first two years of the pandemic have only delayed their original intentions rather than fundamentally changing them. There have been changes, of course, as the need for security, adequate insurance cover, and protection from the collapse of the tour operator have gone to the top of their list when booking a trip. Price is now a little further down the list than previously.

So, the latest WTM research confirms that the most crucial factors previously identified for the mature market are now relevant across all age groups. It is vital that the hospitality and tourism industries use this information to bounce back from a devastating period of restrictive travel.

At the end of January 2022 (gov.uk January 24), the U.K. government released new guidance for COVID-19 testing when coming into the United Kingdom—no testing required at all if you are fully vaccinated. The release noted that it would be welcomed by millions of people desperate to travel restriction-free once more. This was extended still further by March 2022 with the lifting of all travel restrictions. There was lot of support from the travel industry, as you would expect.

Airlines UK hailed it as a landmark for passengers and businesses as it brings "international travel towards near-normality for the fully vaccinated," with added reassurance for anyone planning to travel again. The U.K. Chamber of Shipping also said they were "delighted" the government had eased the restrictions as so many millions of people travel by sea each year. It will bring travel a bit closer to normal, although it may take a bit longer for people to feel confident. As Sarah Treseder said, "this landmark decision will help the tourism and travel sector at a vitally important time for the industry."

As we enter into a period of this new version of normality for travel and tourism globally, it is important to note that COVID-19 still exists whether as a pandemic or as a lesser endemic status. There will need to be recognition of some form of protective measures as we get back to enjoying travel around the world, but everyone is hopeful that the most restrictive measures imposed between 2019 and 2022 will no longer be required. At the time of writing, it is also important to monitor how other political–geographical events may yet introduce more obstacles to safe global tourism.

Reference Sources/ Further Information

Publications

ABTA Travel in 2022 Report. November 2021. www.abta.com/industry-zone/ reports-and-publications/travel-in-2022

ADARA weekly roundup. July 26, 2021. https://go.adara.com/webmail/414092/ 1421720284/4ff37f4c0016dd965712d6e328de2dcd2fb2c4f2db09ad23ddc 09f98267debf5

ADARA US Domestic Business travel trends. November 09, 2021. https://adara .com/ebooks/us-domestic-business-travel-trends/

ADARA—other reports. https://adara.com

- Tourism Rebounding in 2021
- Hotel Rebounding in 2021
- COVID-19 Insight Webinar Series Week 4
- Early 2021 Insights EMEA
- UK Summer Insights August 2021
- Hotel Outlook for summer 2021: Predictions and Strategies (Whitepaper)
- Travel Data Infographic 2022 (summary of points)

Ben Baldanza article—Return of Airline Industry. www.forbes.com/sites/ benbaldanza/2020/12/01/new-study-estimates-up-to-36-of-airline-business-travel-wont-return/?sh=15c5bdc94cf1

Ben Baldanza article—Basis for Future Forecasting. www.forbes.com/sites/ benbaldanza/2021/04/20/two-airline-bellwethers--summer-for-leisure-october-for-business/?sh=3baa37c176ac

Cruise industry statistics report. www.cruisemummy.co.uk/cruise-industry-statistics-facts/

EventMB—Event Manager blog. www.eventmanagerblog.com

Hello! Report "6 ways COVID-19 will change travel in 2021 - expert predictions." www.hellomagazine.com/travel/20210121105131/how-coronavirus-will -change-travel-expert-predictions/

Hubspot/ Talkwalker. 2021. *Social Media Trends Report.* www.hubspot.com

International Travel and Health Insurance Journal (ITIJ). www.itij.com

Jeynes, J. 2021. "Targeting the Mature Traveler: Developing Strategies for an Emerging Market." Business Expert Press. ISBN: 978-1-95253-846-9

Petrova, L. LinkedIn. www.linkedin.com/pulse/time-face-truth-2022-travel-has-become-punishment-liliana-petrova/?fbclid=IwAR2N-DdWqacCrQz-FTKCNVRwpV6GnDtcds61uu6z_GG4Z52-FjHnvK6klQI

Solo Traveler site—https://solotravelerworld.com/about/solo-travel-statistics-data/

Statista World demographics. 2020. "Statista World Demographics 2020." www .statista.com

Statista report. www.statista.com/topics/5966/cruise-industry-in-the-united-kingdom-uk/#dossierKeyfigures

STA. August 2020. "Silver Travel Advisor Travel and Holiday Survey." https:// silvertraveladvisor.com/articles/travel-industry-reports/

STA. May 2020. "Silver Travel Advisor Industry Report." https://silvertraveladvisor .com/articles/travel-industry-reports/

Silver Travel Advisor Industry Report. 2021. https://en.calameo.com/ silvertraveladvisor/read/004427423022c2063a948

The Guardian UK job furlough scheme. August 2021. Report: Opinion—https:// www.theguardian.com/commentisfree/2020/aug/03

Travel Weekly for UK travel industry. https://travelweekly.co.uk/

Travel Weekly report. June 2022. https://travelweekly.co.uk/news/air/britons-say-cost-of-living-concerns-key-barrier-to-foreign-travel

Travel Weekly for US travel industry. www.travelweekly.com

USA Today report. https://traveltips.usatoday.com/advantages-disadvantages-train-travel-39897.html

WishTrip. "Reopening & Running a Destination Post Covid-19." Webinar. www.campaign.wishtrip.com

WP—Washington Post. June 2020. "11 Ways the Pandemic Will Change Travel." www.washingtonpost.com/coronavirus/

Worldometers world demographic. 2020. www.worldometers.info/demographic

World Travel Market. May 2021. Tourism & Biodiversity Friend or Foe blog. https://hub.wtm.com/blog/responsible-tourism/tourism-and-biodiversity-friend-or-foe/

World Travel Market Industry report. 2021. www.wtm.com/content/dam/ sitebuilder/rxuk/wtmkt/documents/WTM-Industry-Report-2021.pdf

Associations

Advantage Travel Partnership—independent travel agent group:

Airlines UK. https://airlinesuk.org/

Airport Operators Association. www.aoa.org.uk

American Hotel and Lodging Association (AHLA). www.ahla.com

Cruise Lines International Association (CLIA). https://cruising.org/en-gb

IATA—International Air Transport Association. www.iata.org

International Civil Aviation Organization. www.icao.int

International Festivals & Events Association (IFEA). www.ifea.com

Silver Marketing Association—previously Mature Marketing Association—Debbie Marshall. https://silvermarketingassociation.org/

UK Chamber of Shipping. www.ukchamberofshipping.com/

UNWTO—United Nations World Travel Organisation. www.unwto.org and www.unwto.org/news/blanket-travel-restrictions-don-t-work-unwto-adds-its-voice-to-who-statement

USTA—US Travel Association. 2021. www.ustravel.org

Travel and Hospitality Providers

Airbnb holiday rentals. www.airbnb.co.uk

Brand USA. www.thebrandusa.com

British Airways. www.britishairways.com

Disney Springs—Walt Disney World Resort. www.disneysprings.com

Explore adventure holidays. www.explore.co.uk

JetBlue airline. www.jetblue.com

OL Pejeta Conservancy—nature reserve in Kenya. www.olpejetaconservancy.org/

Saga Holidays. https://travel.saga.co.uk/

Schofields Insurance—including holiday home insurance cover. www.schofields.ltd.uk

SeaWorld Orlando. https://seaworld.com/orlando/

Sentient Jet private travel provider. www.sentient.com

Squaremouth travel insurance provider. www.squaremouth.com

The Forest, Kenya—includes a zip wire and other attractions. http://theforest.co.ke/

Travelocity—booking flights and accommodation. www.travelocity.com

VRBO vacation rentals. www.vrbo.com

Other Reference Sources

Attest consumer research report. August 2021. www.askattest.com

BBC News/ World online for COVID-19 statistics—https://www.bbc.co.uk/news/world-51235105

Boston University. February 2022. "The Brink report by Ellie Murray." www.bu.edu/articles/2022/difference-between-pandemic-and-endemic

Global Rescue. www.globalrescue.com

MOZ—MozCon Marketing Conference in Seattle. https://moz.com/mozcon

Phocuswright—travel research company. www.phocuswright.com/Travel-Research

Pew Research Center, USA. www.pewresearch.org

Social Media Marketing World event. www.socialmediaexaminer.com/smmworld/

Statista—Facebook usage. www.statista.com/chart/5380/facebook-user-engagement/

Statista—Facebook use by teenagers. www.statista.com/chart/26151/teenage-exodus-from-facebook/

Statista—Global tourism industry—statistics & facts. www.statista.com/topics/962/global-tourism/

Travelzoo surveys UK, USA, and worldwide. www.travelzoo.com

Trondent Development Corporation—travel software. www.trondent.com

Unsplash photo images. www.unsplash.com

Government Sources

Centers for Disease Control and Prevention USA (CDC). www.cdc.gov

Federal Aviation Administration—The US department of transportation. www.faa.gov

FPUC scheme. https://portal.ct.gov/DOLUI/FederalPandemicUnemployment CompensationFPUCfaqs

NASA Earth images including pollution in China. www.nasa.gov/content/nasa-earth-images/

ONS (Office for National Statistics). March 2021. "Mapping the Next Stage of COVID-19 Infection Survey." https://blog.ons.gov.uk/2021/03/30/mapping-the-next-stage-of-the-covid-19-infection-survey/

UK Parliament House of Commons Library—Clark, H. November 15, 2021. https://commonslibrary.parliament.uk/

Wales government information. https://gov.wales/

Wales Government information. See issue 166 October 2021/ issue 162. August 2021. https://gov.wales/coronavirus-covid-19-related-statistics-and-research

YouGov surveys in UK. https://yougov.co.uk/

About the Author

Dr. Jacqueline Jeynes, PhD, MBA, BEd(Hons), BA(Hons)

Dr. Jeynes is a member of the British Guild of Travel Writers (BGTW), a travel writer with a focus on mature travel sectors covering tour packages, travel and accommodation, food and wine, theater, and entertainment. She regularly writes reviews for Silver Travel Advisor plus full-scale reports (3,000 words) on particular destinations, hotel chains, and as part of Press Trips for tour operators. Jacqueline is currently working on a series of books on "A Meander Through Wales" using bus, train, and on foot, so directly related to the current move to reduce an individual's carbon footprint.

In 2022, Dr. Jeynes became an inaugural member of the newly launched Silver Marketing Association (SMA), previously the Mature Marketing Association. Her book *Targeting the Mature Traveler: Developing Strategies for an Emerging Market* was published by Business Expert Press in 2021 and is aimed at those involved in travel and tourism sectors. As a member of the Non-Fiction Authors' Association (NFAA), she regularly reviews books by other authors submitted for the NFAA book awards.

A published nonfiction author of 10 titles since 2000, she is also a writer and tutor of distance learning courses, including art history modules for Aberystwyth University and other online courses aimed at smaller enterprises. The first publications were based on her PhD research on health and safety in small firms, with a new updated version *Managing Health and Safety in a Small Business* published by Business Expert Press in 2022.

As a speaker at international conferences for many years, and based on her wide-ranging business experience, Dr. Jeynes represented U.K. women entrepreneurs at the UN Congress on Women in Beijing.

Dr. Jeynes is an art historian and entrepreneur. She loves theatre and the arts, tasting new wines, completing long-distance walks and traveling to new places. Jacqueline lives with her husband Leslie in a pretty harbor town in West Wales, United Kingdom.

For more information on the courses she writes—new ones for 2022 to accompany the book on health and safety—and travel-related research, e-mail: jackiepencoed@gmail.com

See website for details of all the published titles, and sign up to receive the Newsletter about writing, travel, and art: www.jacquelinejeynes.com

Books by the Author:

Targeting the Mature Traveler

Managing Health & Safety

Index

OTHER TITLES IN THE TOURISM AND HOSPITALITY MANAGEMENT COLLECTION

Betsy Bender Stringam, New Mexico State University, Editor

- *Hotel Revenue Management* by Dave Roberts
- *Astrotourism* by Michael Marlin
- *Enhancing Joy in Travel* by Murphy-Berman Virginia
- *Healthy Vines, Pure Wines* by Pamela Lanier and Jessica Nicole Hughes
- *Overtourism* by Helene von Magius Møgelhøj
- *Food and Beverage Management in the Luxury Hotel Industry* by Sylvain Boussard
- *Targeting the Mature Traveler* by Jacqueline Jeynes
- *Hospitality* by Chris Sheppardson
- *Food and Architecture* by Subhadip Majumder and Sounak Majumder
- *A Time of Change in Hospitality Leadership* by Chris Sheppardson

Concise and Applied Business Books

The Collection listed above is one of 30 business subject collections that Business Expert Press has grown to make BEP a premiere publisher of print and digital books. Our concise and applied books are for...

- Professionals and Practitioners
- Faculty who adopt our books for courses
- Librarians who know that BEP's Digital Libraries are a unique way to offer students ebooks to download, not restricted with any digital rights management
- Executive Training Course Leaders
- Business Seminar Organizers

Business Expert Press books are for anyone who needs to dig deeper on business ideas, goals, and solutions to everyday problems. Whether one print book, one ebook, or buying a digital library of 110 ebooks, we remain the affordable and smart way to be business smart. For more information, please visit www.businessexpertpress.com, or contact sales@businessexpertpress.com.

www.ingramcontent.com/pod-product-compliance
Lightning Source LLC
Chambersburg PA
CBHW061331220326
41599CB00026B/5123